PYTHON DATA SCIENCE:

FROM BEGINNER TO EXPERTS ABOUT TECHNIQUES OF DATA MINING, BIG DATA ANALYTICS AND SCIENCE, PYTHON PROGRAMMING AND HOW TO USE THEM IN BUSINESS.

Table of Contents

Introduction

Introduction of the fundamental concepts of data science and its applications

The fundamental concepts of data science include the importance of data science in business and its application. First, you must have an understanding of regression analysis and how the mining process for data sets work, plus the algorithms and tools that will be used daily so one can master the discipline.

Basic Python Programming

Basic Python Programming is a great way to receive an introduction to statistics via application as well as learning about data science. Python presents the basic skill that this field requires to understand it. But, before you can start working with any data, a firm understanding of how it is extracted must also be known. This is how Python is able to represent itself as the basic tool needed for refining and manipulating it all.

From the very first course you take, you should be taught the basic fundamentals for the Python program so that you have a clear understanding of the CVS files and the best way through the many data structures. These core fundamentals include the understanding of querying, t-tests, the process of tabular data, and distributions and sampling.

SQL and Databases

All data that we see today is mostly mined out of databases that have a minimal amount existing in structured forms. An SQL or "Structured Query Language" is a powerful language that is used to communicate with a database so we can understand them, extract the rich data that they hold, and explore every aspect of them to ensure you have the right data for your current problem. Being able to work with SQL, creating instances of databases via the cloud, running queries of SQL, and accessing the many data sets and databases in the real world is a very necessary skill that every data scientist should have.

The Bayesian Approach and Statistics

A person must have some knowledge of statistics in order to fully understand data science. Because statistics being such a broad field, a data scientist must be able to grasp a few concepts of probability theory in order to provide insights that are practical to a company.

This theory needs to be combined with a lot of practice by way of learning the core fundamentals like regression, testing, distribution, the theory of Bayesian probability, and hypothesis. With most ML modules, they are all mostly based on the Bayesian probability models. With the Bayesian, the approach is considered intuitive in that it goes from the probability straight over to data analysis which allows better accounting for uncertainty and for the providing assumptions and statements that are actionable and are practiced.

Chapter 1: Techniques of Algorithmic programming

In order to master the field of data science, you must be able to learn the many ways of solving problems using the algorithmic techniques available. When an algorithm is used, you are able to manipulate the data stored in the data structures. You also need to learn the way that these structures get implemented throughout the various languages in programming, the best way to break down the big problems into smaller ones, and what to expect in return. A lot of strategies are available to learn and design algorithms. These include learning to recursively solve problems, balancing a binary tree, and how a dynamic array gets resized.

How Data Science Helps Business

In business, power is attained through knowledge, and the fuel that the power is created from is the data. Estimates have been made that by the year 2020, the amount of data volume in gigabytes will be more than 45 trillion. So being able to grab a hold of all this data using data science would be a valuable asset to have. With data science, it uses several methods, algorithms, systems, and processes in order to have knowledge extracted from the data available and then having this data leveraged in order to have decisions made.

If you take an approach that is analytical with numbers, statistics, and facts, then you will have a solution that is reasonable and not seemed to be apparent. Due to the insights that are offered from data science, many companies have begun to utilize data science for the decisions that are evidence-based, to better understand customers and promote the training of employees. When investing in data science, you will begin to see a tremendous amount of value increased right from the start in five ways:

Quantifiable Evidence Promotes Better Decision Making

Data must always be available in order for a company to make a decision. Although this is never easy to do because the majority of the data is considered to be unstructured and requires analytic tools to be able to receive ideas based on the data. When the statistics and numbers are pulled through the use of data science, a company can start to create models that can predict and simulate many possibilities.

Along with that, companies will be able to learn the right solution for them to take so they receive the best outcome possible and having logical, best-case scenarios prescribed in order to have performance improved. Also, by having performance metrics analyzed and recorded, a company will be efficient and a lot smarter at decision-making that is based on trends.

Relevant Product Improvement

Using the methodologies of data science will allow you to analyze the market, make competitive comparisons, and explore some historicals of your services or products to determine when the best time to sell them will be. This will help a business to understand their products' function and the way others will be helped by it.

With a constant reflection and analysis that is achieved by data science, it will provide an understanding of the response caused by the market and a company's services and products. As a hard look is taken at a product and the way it is mostly used, you will be able to rethink the way the model you use is offering services that would benefit your customers the most.

Best Talent is Recruited

It can be an exhausting task to recruit the best talent available. But with the help of data science, the recruiting process will be more accurate, and much faster. With the vast amount of available data points towards talent because of databases, job sites, and social media, many businesses can get through these data points by using methods that are analytical to pin-point the best available candidates that meet the qualifications of the job.

When this data is mined on applicants, you are more confident in knowing that the applicants will fit in like family and not only look good in a resume. This plays more importantly in times where you are looking to fill a vacancy very rapidly. Being able to work smarter by using data science will assure you that the vacancy will have the best applicant filling it.

Staff Training

Regardless of having the right kind of staff, it can be daunting as you try to keep the staff updated and informed of company happenings. The use of data science allows you to grab ideas that could be important to your employees. The knowledge that is gained is then inputted into software designed for online knowledge where employees can then access it as the information becomes relevant to their job. As hard data is pulled, it can also provide facts and statistics for all employees. This will ultimately create a team that will have the knowledge to drive the business forward.

Obtaining a Target Audience

It is believed that the amount of data created daily is around 3 billion BGs. With a large amount of data like this, it can seem impossible to collect the most important customer information. For all of the data collected from a customer, it all can be easily analyzed to obtain a better understanding of customers.

When data science is used for the information obtained by customers, you will be able to combine all data points in order to gain insights that will target a specific audience a lot more. This will allow you to provide tailored products and service to groups. These groups can be based on age or income level where the company could then strategize to create certain types of promotions that tailor to those groups. When data science methodologies are implemented in a company, a value can be added instantly through training, recruiting, marketing, and decision making. Being able to analyze these areas will ensure company growth through ways that are strategic.

Data Science in the Real World

In the real world, data science has changed in a tremendous way and has, in some ways, revolutionized different ways for a business to function more efficiently.

Today, it seems like our daily lives are connected to a gadget in one way or another, with a huge amount of data that also seems to emanate from different sources. Because of this, we seem to be faced with challenges in the study and analysis of a high amount of data if we only use traditional tools for data processing. To get past the challenges, there are some solutions available like Hadoop. Many more companies are maximizing the benefits of the data. Companies are now finding out that they too can benefit in a way that will help their growth. There are more and more opportunity's being created in different sectors. Let us take a look at a few of the sectors where data science is playing a good role.

Data Science in the Education Industry

There is a huge flood of information and data streaming from the education system. Although this data solely relates to student information, it also includes data concerning the results, courses, and faculty. Having this data allows us to analyze it in order to gain important insight that will be used to increase the overall effectiveness of educational institutions.

The following are a few fields in education that either have been or can be improved following the analyzing of data.

- **Learning Programs that are Customized and Dynamic**

Having customized programs that are dynamic will benefit many students and are created by using the collected student data showcasing their learning history. This will allow individual results to improve.

- **Course Material Reframed**

Having course material reframed in accordance with all the collected data and based on student learning and monitoring in real-time of a course would be very beneficial to students.

- **Grading Systems**

Many grading systems have been either introduced or advanced due to the analyzing of data.

- **Prediction of Careers**

Having an analysis of student records will let us see the interests, progress, weaknesses, and strengths. It also helps in determining what the most appropriate career choice would be for the student after graduation.

Data Science in Healthcare

The healthcare industry is packed full of data that concerns all types of information pertaining to patient care.

- The data increases cost reduction for various treatments due to lessening the amounts of diagnosis.
- The data can be used to predict any outbreak or possible epidemic and also help in the decision of what proper measures should be taken.
- The data can help to avoid all preventable diseases from occurring by using early detection. This will allow for early treatment and prevent conditions from getting worse.

- Data can help in deciding which medicine is best to be prescribed based on evidence and research on previous results.

Example

There have been many introductions of wearable sensors and devices to the healthcare field and are able to provide feeds in real-time directly to the patient's record. A technology like this is currently available from Apple.

Apple currently provides 3 types of technology for the healthcare field which are the Apple ResearchKit, HealthKit, and CareKit. The goal of these kits is to allow iPhone customers to upload their record information via their phone.

Data Science in Government

No matter which country's government you call yours, there will always be a ton of data available to look at. The reason why is because the governments need to keep track of their citizens by using different types of databases and records including vital statistics, geographics and surveys, and population growth.

All of this data is important, and with the proper analysis and study, can help a government tremendously in the following ways:

Welfare Services

- Decisions are made faster concerning different social and welfare programs.
- Areas are identified as having immediate attention needed.
- Monitoring agriculture and keeping updated data concerning livestock and agricultural land.
- Being able to withstand challenges and decrease the risk of energy exploitation, terrorism, and unemployment.

Cyber Security

- Data science plays a major role in detecting and recognizing deceit.
- It can be implemented to detect tax evasion.

Example

The FDA, under federal guidelines, benefits from data science by analyzing data that could detect patterns so that food sources can be monitored efficiently in case of mass food contamination.

Data Science in Media and Entertainment

With many people owning at least one piece of digital technology, a ton of data can only occur because of it. This makes it the number one reason for the increase in data.

Besides that, many of the social media outlets provide an alternate way to collect data. Many businesses in these industries have figured out the importance of this data, so benefiting from it has become second nature.

Benefits of science data in media and entertainment

- Audience interests are predicted efficiently.
- All media streams are optimized for distribution through media and digital platforms.
- Insights are obtained through reviews.
- Advertisements effectively target the consumer.

Example

The on-demand music giant, Spotify, uses data science and analytics by collecting subscriber data. Then after analyzing the data, they are able to create recommendations to the individual users.

Chapter 2: The Database Access with Python

There are times when you are going to want to work with Python in order to access a database and to get through all of the information that is found inside of it. There are a lot of databases that are needed in order to make sure our information is put in the right place, that you can keep track of all the information, and so much more. Learning how to bring Python into the database, no matter what you are doing with it, can make a big difference in the results that you are able to get.

The Python standard that is used when being with a database will be Python DB-API. Most of the interfaces that are used with Python databases are going to adhere to this kind of standard so it needs to be something that you should learn about. You can always choose the database for the application that you are working on. Python Database API is going to support a lot of different database servers, which makes it easier for you to pick the one that you would like to use. Some of the options that work well for this include:

1. GadFly

2. mySQL

3. Sybase

4. Oracle

5. Interbase

6. Informix

7. Microsoft SQL Server 2000

8. PostgreSQL

9. MySQL

Keep in mind here that you need to go through and download out a separate DB API module for each of the databases that you should access. So if you need to change the API that you are working with, then you will need to list out a different module to make it work. For example, if you need to go through and work with both the MySQL database and the Oracle database, you need to download both modules for both of these.

You will find that the DB API is going to provide a minimum standard for working with database in Python and you have to work with the Python syntax and structures when it is possible. The API is going to include a few different things that can help you to get the work done including:

1. It can import the API module that you want to work with.

2. It can help to acquire a connection over to the database that you want to work with.

3. It can help to issue the statements in SQL and the stored procedures.

4. It can help to close out the connection.

Handling some of the errors

There are going to be times when your database access with Python is not going to go as well as you would hope. There are a lot of sources for these errors and knowing what they all mean can be important. Some of the different errors that can show up in this kind of work could be when you call the fetch method for a statement handle that is finished or canceled, a connection failure, an executed SQL statement that has a syntax error, and more. There are a few different types of exceptions that you can handle when doing a database, and some of the most common ones that you are most likely going to see, and their meanings, will include:

□□   Warning: This one is going to be used for issues that are going to be non-fatal. It is going to be with the subclass of the StandardError.

□□   Error: This is going to be the base class that comes up with most of the errors that show up in the code.

□□   InterfaceError: This one is going to be used when there are some errors that show up in the module for the database, rather than in the database on its own.

□□   **DatabaseError: This one is going to be used when the error that you are dealing with is going to show up in the actual database.**

□□   DataError: This is going to be one of the subclasses that you are going to see with the DatabaseError and it is going to tell you that some of your data has an error.

□□   OperationalERror: This is going to be another part of the subclass of a DatabaseError that will refer to any of the errors that can be outside of the control of Python

and the programmer who is using it. It could include something like losing the connection with your database.

☐☐ IntegrityError: This is going to be another subclass that can handle situations that would end up damaging the relationship integrity that shows up in the database, including the uniqueness constraints that you try to use or some of the foreign keys.

☐☐ InternalError: This is going to be part of the DatabaseError and it is going to refer to any of the errors that happen internally in the module of the database. This could include having it so that the cursor is no longer active and useable.

☐☐ ProgrammingError: This is going to be a part that will refer to the errors that are there, such as a bad name for the table, and some of the things that can be safely blamed on the programmer instead of on something else in the process.

☐☐☐ NotSupportedErorr: This is going to be a part that is going to show up when you want to call up some kind of functionality that is unsupported.

The scripts that you are able to write out in Python are going to help to handle some of these errors. However, before you try to use any of the exceptions that are able or try to handle any of them, make sure that the MySQLdb that you are using has the support to handle it. You can go through and read the specifications to figure out if you are able to do this or not.

Chapter 3: What Can I Do with GUI Programming?

The next topic that we are going to spend some time on is the idea of the GUI or graphical user interface. This is one of the methods that you can use for programming, and Python is going to help us to get it all done. This kind of interface is going to have a bunch of interactive components, including icons and other graphical objects that can make sure that a user can interact with any kind of computer software that you would like, including the operating system on the computer.

The GUI is a useful tool to learn about because it is considered one of the most user-friendly out of all the others, rather than using a command-line interface that is based on text, including the shell that we find with the Unix operating systems, or MS-DOS. You can think about this as the little icons on your computer. If you spend your time just clicking on icons to open up things on your computer rather than opening up a command line and typing in a code to get things done, then you are working with the GUI programming.

The GUI system was first developed by Douglas Engelbart, Alan Kay, and other researchers at Xerox PARC in 1981. Later, Apple started to introduce the Lisa computer that had this GUI in it in 1983. Let's take a look at some of the different things that we need to know when it comes to GUI programming and will be able to help understand how this is going to work better and why we need to work with this kind of interface.

To start with this, we need to take a look at how the GUI works. This is going to use a lot of different options including menus, icons, and windows in order to help you to carry out the different commands that come up. There are a lot of commands that you are able to use with this kind of interface, including moving, deleting, and opening the files. Although this kind of operating system is going to be used in most cases with a mouse, you can also work with the keyboard to make this happen with the arrow keys or some of the shortcuts on the keyboard that are there.

Let's look at an example that comes with this. If you would like to use the GUI system in order to open up a program, you would need to take the mouse pointer and move it the icon for the program that you want. And then just double click from there and the computer will know the work that you want it to do. Your program will work and can help you to open up the program and use it for your needs.

There are a lot of benefits to working with this GUI programming, especially when you are the user of a computer. Most people do not know enough about coding in order to open up the command line and get the right program to work for them. This makes it hard for them to navigate around a computer they want to use. But with GUI, this problem is going to be solved and can help anyone to use a computer, just by recognizing which icon they need to click on to get what they want out of everything on the computer.

Unlike some of the operating systems that are going to use the command line, known as CUI, which is found with the MS-DOS and Unix systems. GUI operating systems can be a lot easier to learn and a lot easier to use because you don't have to know and memorize the different commands that are available. In addition, you will be able to use this kind of system without needing to know how to use any kind of programming language at all.

This is something that a lot of computer users are going to like. The GUI is going to make it easier to use the computer, even if your use of computers and your knowledge of how to run a coding language is limited, then the GUI system is going to be the right one for you to use. Because of the ease of use that comes with this kind of system, and the appearance that is more widely accepted and modern, these systems are pretty much dominating the market for computers and coding that are out there.

Most of the modern operating systems that you want to use are going to work with the idea of GUI. Windows computers, most of the newer Apple computers, Chrome OS, and a lot of the variants of Linux will rely on this as well. And there are going to be a lot of examples that we are looking at that will work with the GUI interface including Firefox, Chrome, Internet Explorer, any of the programs with Microsoft, KDE, and GNOME.

The next question that you may have is how a user is going to be able to interact with the GUI. Most of the time, it is going to be doable with a mouse to interact with almost all of the aspects of the GUI. In some of the more modern devices, especially with mobile, it is possible to use a touchscreen to get it done. It is also possible, in some cases, to work with a keyboard, but most people are going to rely on either the mouse or the touchscreen in order to pick out what they want to do on their computer.

Users who are not familiar with GUI or GLI may want to learn a bit more about these and how they are going to work and how each is different. Even though we are used to working with the GUI because it just includes clicking on the icon on your screen and the information will open up and be ready for you to use, there are times when working with the command line can be the better option, especially based on the kind of project you want to work with. Let's take a look at some of the comparison that you can see between GUI and CLI and how you would be able to benefit from each one.

Topic	CLI	GUI
Ease of Use	Because there is going to be more memorization and the familiarity that is needed to operate and navigate on this system, many new users are going to find that it is harder to work with the CLI than it is the GUI.	Because this kind of interface is intuitive visually, many users find that it is faster and easier to work with the GUI rather than the CLI.
Control	Users are going to have a lot of control when it comes to the operating system and the file in the CLI. However, for someone who is new and hasn't used this method, it is not going to be as friendly for users.	The GUI is going to offer a lot of access to the files, the operating system, and the software features as a whole. This method is going to be seen as more user-friendly than the command line option and it is going to be used more often than the CLI.
Multitasking	Although many of the environments for command line are capable of multitasking, they are not going to offer us with the same kind of easy ability in order to see more than one thing on the same screen.	GUI users are going to be able to work with a window that helps the users to toggle, manipulate, control, and view through more than one program and folder at the same time.

Speed	The users of the command line will only have to rely on their keyboard in order to navigate around the interface, which gives them some faster performance in the process.	While GUIs are often efficient and fast, they are going to require the use of the mouse. This is going to be a bit slower than what we are going to see with the CLI.
Resources	For the CLI, a computer that is only going to use the command line takes less time and less of the resources of the computer compared to the GUI.	The GUI is going to take more system resources because of the elements that have been shown with loading, including the fonts and icons. Things like video and mouse need to be loaded up, taking up additional resources on the system.
Scripting	A command-line interface is mostly going to require the users to already know a bunch of different commands for scripting and the syntax that comes with it. This can make it hard for a new or a novice user to create some scripts.	Creating a script with the GUI is easier thanks to some of the modern programming software. This is going to make it easier to write the scripts without having to know all of the syntax ad the commands. This software is also going to provide guides and tips for how to code some of the functions that you need.

Remote access	When you use CLI to access another device or computer on the same network, the user is going to be able to use this interface in order to manipulate the device and any files. You do need to know how to do all of this and which commands to use so it is harder for a beginner.	You will find that this interface makes it easier to remotely access another server or computer, and it is easy to navigate, even when you don't have a lot of experience. IT professionals like to work with GUI for some remote access that they need, including the management of user computers and servers.
Diversity	After you have been able to learn how to properly work with the command line, there is not much that will change with it. The new commands can be introduced to this on occasion but the original commands are going to stay the same over time.	Each GUI is going to have a different design and a different structure when you want to perform different tasks. Even when you have an iteration of the same GUI, it is possible that there are a lot of changes with all of the versions.
Strain	The CLI is going to be pretty basic and this can be the cause of more strain on the user's vision. Using the keyboard is not that preferable to a lot of users	The use of things like shortcut keys and more frequent movement of hand positions due to switching between the mouse and the keyboard, which can reduce the strain

either. You have to watch your posture and pay attention to how you are using the wrists and fingers in the right manner.

that comes with using it. Visual strain can still be something of a risk, but there are more colors with GUI and it is more appealing visually so this issue is not as big as it can be with the CLI.

Working with the GUI is definitely something that we are familiar with on most of the computers that we use. Unless you are planning on getting a computer that can just help you to create a program or do coding with, you will find that the GUI is going to be present on the computer. This makes life easier for a lot of users because they just have to go through and click on the icon that they want to use, and they are taken right there.

This has been done in order to cut out some of the work that is needed to reach the different parts that come with the computer and to open up the software and the applications that you have there. This may take out some of the codings that you need to do, but it does make it easier for those who don't know how to code on their own, and who don't have any experience with coding, get things done in the process.

Think about the last computer that you worked on and how it looked. When you started it up, did it have a lot of little icons for the Internet of choice, for Word, and for the other documents and programs that you wanted to use? Or did it have a command line show up and you were expected to type in some kind of code in order to open up any application on the computer? If your computer has some of the first part present, then this is a sign that you are working with the GUI, but if you see the second one, you are working with the CLI.

Both of these have some positives and negatives to work with, but knowing how they work, what you are able to do with each of them, and having a better understanding of when you would want to use each of them is going to be pivotal when you are working on your own coding.

If you would like to do more with coding, rather than relying on the GUI and the graphs that are there, you may want to work with the CLI option so that you are able to write out some of the different parts that come with your own coding as well. But you can definitely work with the idea of the GUI if you find that this is easier to work with and will meet your needs in this process as well.

Chapter 4: Recent Advancements in Data Analysis

Machine learning has changed drastically since its beginning in 1959 with Arthur Samuel's checkers playing computer. But it has changed more in the last two decades than in its entire history, especially with the improvement of computing power. In the past, machine learning and big data analysis used to be very limited. Only larger companies with expensive tech had the ability to use data to make business decisions.

Now, almost anyone can utilize some amount of data for business or other purposes with a laptop or home computer. Data is much easier to come by, and the machines to process it have also become much more accessible. What used to take expensive computing power can now be done much more cheaply, and quicker.

The advent of cloud technology has made it easier for smaller businesses access to large datasets without the need for massive amounts of data storage. Now machine learning has become a completely different field of computer science, with people who specialize in machine learning and data science as its own field.

More and more things are connected nowadays, and the internet continues to grow larger and larger all the time. This means that access to data is increasing, but also the sources of data are changing. Even people's cars have computers in them, which means that when they drive, they are creating data which can be interpreted. The vast majority of Americans carry a cell phone and do internet shopping and use apps for navigation. People use their phones to control home appliances, which is another potential source of data. There are Fitbits and smartwatches which allow people to track data about their health.

The more devices, not just computers, and phones, but devices of all kinds, are connected, the greater the possibilities in terms of collecting and studying data. This connection of everything; smartphones, smart cars, etc. make people nervous that they may be at risk of losing their private data. They fear that their privacy at stake and someone is always watching them. But machine learning and data analytics are making our lives much easier. Finding the right products is easier, navigation is easier, and finding new music is easier. This is all thanks to machine learning.

Image Recognition

One of the applications of machine learning models is for the sorting and classification of data. This type of classification can even be used for the classification of images. Search engines use this kind of algorithm to identify photos, and social media sites now use face detection to identify a person in a photo before the photo is even tagged. They do this by learning from data compiled from other photos. If your social media account can recognize your face in a new photo, this is because it has created models using data from all the other photos on your account.

Image recognition techniques require deep learning models. Deep learning models are made with an artificial neural network, which will be covered more extensively later in this book. Deep learning is the most complex type of machine learning in which data is filtered through several hidden layers of nodes. They are called hidden layers because the models are unsupervised, meaning that the features identified by the model are not chosen by the data scientist beforehand. Usually, the features are patterns that the model identifies on its own. Features identified in neural networks can be quite complicated, the more complicated that the task is the more layers that the model will have. Image sorting models might only have two or three layers, while self-driving cars will have between one and two hundred hidden layers.

We have made big strides in this in recent years, because of the increased availability of computing power. Imagine the computing power that it requires to pass thousands of data points through hundreds of stacked nodes simultaneously. Deep learning and artificial neural networks have become more feasible in the last decade, with the improvement of computers and the reduction of cost to process large amounts of data. Especially with the advent of the cloud, which allows data scientists to have access to huge amounts of data without using physical storage space.

There is a website called ImageNet, which is a great resource for data scientists interested in photo classification and neural networks. ImageNet is a database of images that is publicly accessible for use in machine learning. The idea is that by making it publicly accessible, the improvement of machine learning techniques will be a cooperative effort with data scientists around the world.

ImageNet's database has around 14 million photos in its database, with more than 21,000 possible class groups. This allows a world of possibilities for data scientists to be able to access and classify photos to learn and experiment with neural networks.

Each year, ImageNet hosts a competition for data scientists worldwide to create new models for image classification. Each year the competition gets harder. Now they are starting to transition to classifying videos instead of images, which means that the complexity and level of processing power required will continue to grow exponentially. Using the millions of photographs in the database, the ImageNet competition has fostered groundbreaking strides in image recognition made during the last few years.

Modern photo classification models require methods capable of very specific classification. Even if two images should be put in the same category, they may look very different. How do you make a model that can distinguish between them?

Take, for example, these two different photos of trees. If you were creating a neural network model that classified images of trees, then ideally you would want your model to categorize both as photos of trees. A human can recognize that these are both photos of trees, but the features of the photo would make them very difficult to classify with a machine learning model.

The fewer differences the variables have, the easier they are to classify. If all your photos of trees looked like the image on the left, with the tree in full view with all its features, then the model would be easier to make. Unfortunately, this would lead to overfitting, and when the model is introduced to data with photos like the one on the right, your model wouldn't be able to classify it properly. We want our model to be capable of classifying our data, even when they aren't as easy to classify.

Incredibly, ImageNet has been able to make models capable of classifying data with many variables, and very similar data. Recently, they created Image recognition that can even identify and categorizes photos with different breeds of dog. Imagine all the variables and the similarities that the model would need to recognize in order to tell the difference between dog breeds properly.

The challenge of identifying commonalities between a class is known as Intra-class variability. When we have a picture of a tree stump and a photo of a tree silhouetted in a field, we are dealing with intra-class variability. This problem is how variables within the same class can differ from each other, making it harder for our model to predict which category they fall in to properly. Most importantly, it requires a lot of data over time to improve the model and make it accurate.

In order to have an accurate model despite high levels of intra-class variability, we will need to use additional techniques with our neural network models to find patterns among images. One method involves the use of convolutional neural networks. Rather than having just one model or algorithm, data is fed through several models which are stacked on top of each other. The neural networks convert images features into numerical values to sort them.

Unfortunately, it would be beyond the scale of this book to try and understand the way these deep neural networks operate, but there are many books available that cover those types of models and also include more comprehensive explanations of the coding required to perform these types of analysis.

Speech Recognition

Improvements in artificial intelligence have made speech recognition more useful very recently. Most of our smartphones now have some level of speech recognition ability, which involves machine learning. Speech recognition takes the audio data we give it, and it turns it into text that can be interpreted.

The difficult thing about speech recognition is the irregularities in the way that people speak. Like intra-class variability. You and I may have different accents and different inflections that are hard to account for when you are teaching a computer how to understand the human voice.

If we both say the same word with different accents, how do we teach the model to understand us?

Speech recognition also uses neural networks to interpret data, like image recognition. This is because the patterns in audio data would probably not be recognizable by a human. Data scientists use sampling in order to interpret data and make accurate predictions despite the variances in peoples voices. Sampling is done by measuring the height and length of the sound waves, which believe it or not can be used to decipher what the user is saying. The recorded audio is converted into the wave map of frequencies. Those frequencies are measured by numerical values and then fed through the neural networks hidden layers to look for patterns.

Medicine and Medical Diagnosis

Machine learning is not just useful for digital marketing or making computers respond to your requests. It also has the potential to improve the field of medicine, particularly in the diagnosis of patients using data from previous patients.

With as much potential as machine learning has for medical diagnosis, it can be challenging to find patient data that is available to use for machine learning because of the laws surrounding patient privacy. Its gradually gaining acceptance in the field of medicine, which means data is becoming available to data scientists. Unfortunately, up until now, it has been difficult to have enough meaningful data to be able to make models regarding medical diagnosis. But the technology is there and available to be used.

Machine learning could use image recognition to diagnose x-rays by taking data from several patients to imaging scans in order to make predictions about new patients. Clustering and classification can be used to categorize different types of the same disease so that patients and medical professionals can have better a better understanding of the variation of the same disease between two patients, and their likelihood of survival.

Medical diagnosis with machine learning can reduce diagnosis errors made by doctors or give the doctors something to offer them a second opinion. It can also be used to predict the probability of a positive diagnosis based on patient factors and disease features. Someday, medical professionals may be able to look at data from thousands of patients about a certain disease to make a new diagnosis.

But medical diagnosis is just one of the numerous ways that machine learning could be utilized in medicine. Medical datasets remain small today, and the science of machine learning still has a lot of unmet potential in the field of medicine.

Chapter 5: Python Data Structures

Data structures are collections of one or more data types that are assembled in such a way to make data easy to manipulate. To some degree, even data types like integers can be called data structures, however, we will not argue about the details.

Data structures are one of the most important categories of programming elements because they include lists, tuples, and dictionaries among a few others. These are data types which you will frequently use when handling data because there are a number of operations designed to manipulate it.

Lists

Lists are one of the most simple but handy data structures you can manipulate. You can change any of the elements in a variety of ways, you can store various data types and other structures, you can customize its size and so on. It's worth mentioning that Python lists are similar to the array in other programming languages such as C. Furthermore, they are in some ways similar to strings because you can perform any string operation on a list as well. Here's an example of a list:

x = [1, 2, 3, 4, 5, 6, 7, 8, 9, 10]

As you can see, lists are declared by using square brackets []. This is the most basic kind of list that contains only one type of data, namely integers. Keep in mind that the same list can contain multiple data types. Here's an example:

book = ["title", 1, 2, 3, "42"]

Next, you can perform a variety of string operations, such as concatenations. The same way you can concatenate two strings, you can concatenate two lists. Let's apply this operation on the two lists we created:

x + book

The result will be a concatenation of the two lists:

[1, 2, 3, 4, 5, 6, 7, 8, 9, 10, "title", 1, 2, 3, "42"]

Next, let's discuss dictionaries.

Dictionaries

Imagine dictionaries like going through the yellow pages, or through a search engine that has information about any phone number you want as long as you know the name of the person you want to contact. In this example, the name would be the key, and the data (the phone number) is represented by values. The key represents the data and it can only be a string, a number or a tuple. This means that the key is not mutable. Values, on the other hand, can contain any kind of data, and the dictionaries themselves are mutable, therefore you can change them. Dictionary keys and values can be edited and manipulated.

On a side note, if you are experienced with any other programming language, you should know that dictionaries are the same as hashes or associative arrays. This similarity is helpful in determining the fact that dictionary keys are just hashed values. This means that a hashed key can store another key in the form of a value that is taken from the main key. You are probably confused by now, however, all you should know is that Python uses the hashed key in order to organize a dictionary's data. The data is not managed alphabetically. This means that when you change a value you also obtain a changed hash.

Enough theory for now. Let's see how to create a simple dictionary by typing the following lines:

dict = {'fruit' : 'apple', 'vegetable' : potato'}

dict ['vegetable']

As you can see, the values come paired with a key. The data is separated from the key with a colon and they are all defined inside braces instead of brackets or parentheses. The result from our example will be "potato" because we called its key. Don't forget that the key can also be a number or anything else. It doesn't have to be a string like in this case.

As you can probably conclude on your own, dictionaries are excellent choices for storing attributes and values. For example, you can use one to determine all the states which a certain object can be in. This is possible because the key is always unique. Therefore, the values will be unique for that key and you won't end up with repeating results. For instance, if you want to learn the number of times a specific character appears in a paragraph, you can assign every single character to a key and then go from there.

Tuples
This data structure is nearly identical to a list, except that you cannot edit it later in your code after you declare it. In other words, it is an immutable data structure which contains data items ordered in a specific way and they are locked inside a container. You can look at tuples as lists that contain values. They are separated by commas and declared inside parentheses instead of brackets or braces. As you can see, the type of enclosure you use will define what data type or structure a variable represents, so make sure you always use the correct one. However, it is worth mentioning that in case of tuples the parentheses are not obligatory. You should still use them though, because they are considered standard practice and they can help avoid any unnecessary confusion.

Furthermore, tuples can contain any type of value. You can combine them as much as you want. You can even declare a collection of tuples inside your tuple, or nothing at all. Let's start by declaring an empty tuple:

emptyTuple = ()

Now let's add a data type:

myTuple = ('element')

Their purpose does not involve data manipulation or editing. Tuples are used when you need to pass a value to an object, without modifying the original state of the value. The tuple guarantees that the original form is maintained. If you need the ability to change the value, then use the list instead.

The Matrix

Take the red pill and start learning about multidimensional lists. A matrix is essentially a collection of lists inside another list and it is presented like a table which holds the data items. Let's take a look at an example:

myMatrix = [[11, 12, 13], [21, 22, 23], [31, 32, 33]]

A matrix is defined by its size, or the number of elements it contains. In this case we have a 3 x 3 matrix.

Keep in mind that in order to access the elements inside a list it is recommended that you work with for loops. Sometimes you have to work with lists of an unknown size and the for loop will iterate automatically through all the elements even if you don't know how many there are. Keep it simple and let the system work for you, not against you. Since matrices are somewhat similar to lists, you can use a for loop again with the same principle. However, you will have to use nested for loops instead, meaning a for loop inside another for loop.

Chapter 6: Numba - Just In Time Python compiler

Although numpy is written in C or Fortran and standard routines working on arrays of data are highly optimized, non-standard operations are still coded in python and might be painfully slow. Fortunately, the Pydata company developed a package that can translate python code into native machine code on the fly and execute it at the same speed as C programs. In some respects, this approach is even better than compiled code because the resulting code is optimized for each particular machine and can take advantage of all the features of the processor, whereas regular compiled programs might ignore some processor features for the sake of compatibility with older machines, or might have even been compiled before new features were even developed.

Besides, your Python program, using the Numba just in time compiler will work on any platform for which Python and Numba are available. The user will not need to worry about C compiler. There will be no hassle with dependencies or complex makefiles and scripts. Python code just works out of the box - taking full advantage of all available hardware.

The LLVM virtual machine used by Numba allows compiled code to run on different processor architectures, GPU, and accelerator boards. It is under heavy development, so while I was writing this book execution times for example programs were cut more than in half.

Such heavy development on both Numba and LLVM has some disadvantages as well. Obviously, some Python features could never be significantly accelerated. But some could and will be accelerated in future versions of Numba. When I started working on this book, Numba's compiled functions could not handle lists or create numpy arrays. Now, they can do it. Obviously, some material in this section will be obsolete well before the rest of the book. But it is a good thing. Just keep an eye on Pydata's NUMBA web site.

For some strange reason, numba was not included in the Anaconda Linux installer. So, I had to install it manually by opening anaconda3/bin folder in terminal and typing

conda install numba

The same should work on windows. Just use terminal shortcut from Anacomda's folder in Windows start menu. Numba is usually included with later versions of winpython. If not, download the wheel package and dependence packages from <u>CHRISTOPHER GOHLKE'S PAGE</u> and install them using winpython's setup utility.

To illustrate speedups you can get with <u>numba</u>, I'll implement the Sieve of Eratosthenes prime number search algorithm. Because, in order to accelerate a function, <u>Numba</u> needs to know the type of all the variables or at least should be able to guess them, and this type should not change during function. The execution <u>numpy</u> arrays are the data structures of choice when working with <u>numba</u>.

Here is the Python code:

```
fromnumbaimport jit

import numpy as np

import time

@jit('i4(i4[:])')

defget_primes(a):
    m=a.shape[0]

    n=1

    foriin range(2,m):
        ifa[i]==0:
```

```python
        n+=1

    for j in range(i*2,m,i):

        a[j]=0

    return n

#create an array of integers 0 to a million
a=np.arange(10000000, dtype=np.int32)

start_time = time.time()  #get system time

n=get_primes(a)           #count prime numbers

#print number of prime numbers below a million

#and execution time
print(n,time.time()-start_time)
```

First, we import numba, numpy, and the time module that will be used to time the program execution. Then, we need a function implementing the Sieve of Eratosthenes on numpy's array of integers. A function's definition is preceded by the decorator@jit (Just In Time compile) imported from the numba package. It tells numba to compile this function into machine code. The rest of the program is executed as plain Python. Decorator tells numba that function must return a four bite or 32 bit integer, and receives a parameter that is one dimensional array of 4 byte integers.

Using numpy'sarange function, we can create an array of consecutive integer numbers between zero and a million, remember current time. Call up a functionget_primes that counts the prime numbers in the array and zeroes out non-prime numbers. As soon as the function returns, we get current time again and print the number of found prime numbers as well as time function was executing.

On my Sandy Bridge laptop, numba accelerated function takes about 7ms to complete. If I comment out @jit decorator -

#@jit('i4(i4[:])')

The execution time increases to 3s. Compilation results in 428 fold speedup. Not bad for one line of code. Searching for prime numbers between 1 and 10 millions takes 146ms with numba and 42s in pure Python respectively. This is also 287 fold speedup. These numbers are bound to change as numba, llvm, and processors improve.

Because the function get_primes gets just a reference and nota copy of the original array, non-prime numbers in the array are still zeroed out and we can get prime numbers using the fancy indexing discussed in the numpy section:

PRINT*aa0*

Default array printing behavior is not particularly useful here as it only shows a few numbers at the beginning and the end of the array. You can change this behavior or just iterate through a filtered array usingfor loop.

Troubleshooting numba functions

Although numba is under heavy development and is quickly becoming more robust, it is still a tool for optimizing the most critical parts of code. These parts should be refactored in small functions, debugged in plain Python, and then decorated with numba's@jit decorator.

In the best case scenario, you will instantly see a performance boost. But, sometimes you see no difference. It is likely that numba failed to compile the function into machine codes and falls back on using Python's objects to represent problematic variables. This slows execution down to almost a pure Python level. Perhaps, in some cases, it is good that the function doesn't fail completely, but it doesn't report problems either and you don't know if you can tweak your code a little to get your two orders of magnitude performance increase.

One way to force the compilation to machine code is by the giving@jitdecorator a parameternopython=True. This will force numba to fail compilation and show an error message if any variable could not be compiled into the processor's native type. Another approach is to set the environmental variableNUMBA_WARNINGS before importing numba. You can do this from within your python script by adding two lines on top of it.

import os

os.environ['NUMBA_WARNINGS']="1"

from numba import @jit

Finally, you can dump numba's intermediate representation of your function by applying a methodinspect_typesto your numba compiled functions. If any variable has typepyobjectinstead of something likeint32orfloat64, there might be a problem. As numba is getting smarter, the impact of this problem outside of tight loops might diminish dramatically, but, on the other hand, the problematic parts of code that can easily reduce performance several fold become harder to spot.

Describing the types of function parameters, return value, and local variables in@jitdecorator might also significantly increase the performance of your numba-compiled function. You might play with some additional numba compilation parameters. For instance, the use of AVX commands is disabled on Sandy bridge and Ivy bridge processors by default, and you might want to try enabling it. This could be done by setting an environment variableNUMBA_ENABLE_AVX. In case you are curious to see the assembly code of your numba compiled function, you may request numba to print it for you by setting the environmental variableNUMBA_DUMP_ASSEMBLY.

import os

os.environ['NUMBA_ENABLE_AVX']="1"

os.environ['NUMBA_DUMP_ASSEMBLY']="1"

from numba import @jit

See NUMBA DOCUMENTATION for more details.

Chapter 7: Comparing Pipeline Data Models: Is PODS Spatial the Right Solution?

Distinctive pipeline information models offer various advantages and difficulties with regards to information stockpiling and access. The latest technology, the PODS Spatial (ESRI Spatial 5.0 geodatabase), due to be discharged for open use toward the beginning of September 2010, is the consequence of numerous redesigns and upgrades to the essential PODS model and can be the ideal mix of other existing arrangements.

Indeed, the principal grievance of numerous associations utilizing the essential PODS model is the trouble with spatially empowering this model and the rigidity that outcomes from this weakness. The latest manifestation of the Pipeline Open Data Standard Spatial comes in two particular variants, one that is situated in Oracle Spatial technology technology. and another that

This section will is situated in ESRI geodatabase concentrate on the ESRI Spatial

adaptation (additionally referred to and broadly alluded to as the PODS Spatial).

The PODS Spatial geodatabase is intended to unite the absolute best highlights of the APDM ideas while remaining gauges based. Somehow or another it very well may be viewed as a nearby relative of that pipeline information model, on account of its usage of a class progression and legacy framework for information. The PODS Spatial keeps on being a guidelines based model, while the APDM isn't. Customarily, the PODS social model offers occasion tables, and this technology is reliable in the Pipeline Open Data Standard Spatial variant. This makes the PODS Spatial a happy medium between the standard PODS model and the APDM frameworks.

Your association might search for a PODS Spatial arrangement if:

• ESRI geodatabase technology is as of now set up

• Relational information uprightness is to be kept up through application rationale.

• SOA technology is as of now set up and being utilized

• Your association favors a guidelines based information model.

• ArcGIS is the spatial mapping technology that is utilized.

• Being ready to use a wide range of ESRI-based applications and outsider apparatuses is significant.

At long last, there are a few decisions with regards to pipeline information models. This is anything but a "one size fits all" sort of issue, so having alternatives is significant. Picking the best model to fit the necessities of your organization will rely upon a few components, and cautious survey of the PODS, APDM, and PODS Spatial choices is significant before settling on any decision.

Giving Data Modelers something to do

When dealing with a Data Governance program, there are a few things that are basic to your prosperity. Measurements are one of these - you should most likely show where you were, the place you are going, and what you have achieved. If you can't do this, good karma getting official purchase in!

A development model by and important positions your information on a 1-5 scale. A 1, for the most part, implies you have no power over it, and a 5, for the most part, means you have full authority over it.

Presently, how would you like to follow these development levels? You could dump all your in extension field names into one more spreadsheet and after that track them in Excel... or on the other hand, what about this... have your Data Modelers follow it in their information displaying apparatus!

What we did was we added another credit to fields called development level. At that point, in that field, we relegate the number that the area presently lives at. You would then be able to do cool stuff like force all dimension one information, or all dimension five information, or anything short of level 3.

This is an extremely integral asset that is ignored, influence your information modelers!!!

Contrasting Pipeline Data Models - Is APDM the Right Solution?

With a few decisions for pipeline information models, contrasting each sort can enable you to discover which type would be best for your association's needs. While the standard kind of pipeline information model (Pipeline Open Data Standard, PODS) is a solid match for some associations, numerous others will require new or various highlights, which might be found inside the ArcGIS Pipeline Data Model (APDM).

There are a few eminent contrasts between the APDM and PODS models. Significantly, the APDM is dependent upon specific ESRI ArcGIS technology, while PODS is viewed as GIS-impartial. Hence, when you are looking for a pipeline information answer for an association that does not go to utilize ArcGIS, at that point, the APDM won't be a viable arrangement.

The APDM is utilized inside a Relational Database Management System (RDBMS) as an ESRI Geodatabase model. RDBMS models, for example, Oracle or Microsoft SQL Server are perfect with this execution. While the geodatabase is contained inside the RDBMS, note that it isn't wholly a social database. The impacts of this distinction include:

• Typically, Structured Query Language (SQL) won't be as dependable while getting to or controlling information in this kind of database

• Relational uprightness isn't carefully implemented, regardless of the way that the geodatabase uses relationship classes and code spaces.

While there are a few restrictions to the APDM pipeline information model, there are likewise extra highlights and capacities that can be appealing to individual associations, for example,

• Longer transaction ability

• Archiving and following of history

• Geometric systems take into consideration better topology the board.

• No extra software is essential to empower the APDM spatially

Given the implicit article social structure, the APDM permits information displaying to happen using the idea of legacy. This makes a class chain of command: all classes toward the finish of the "legacy tree" consequently utilize the substance of all branches coming in front of them. (Unique courses are the "progenitors" for this situation.) Their legacy additionally arranges all tables and highlight records. This takes into account simpler information, arranging and understanding.

Since the APDM model uses the more unique class classifications that are permitted through the idea of legacy, the APDM successfully turns into a layout based model that has far greater adaptability than is usually found in the standard PODS model. APDM additionally takes into account greater customization for an association, with fewer software modifications required from outside sellers.

While ESRI geodatabase technology utilizes SQL information get to, this isn't a consistent procedure. Some high transaction efficiency is ultimately compromised in this procedure. One likely answer to this lack is utilizing Service Oriented Architecture (SOA). An SOA takes into account the utilization of different web benefits, and, joined with the ESRI ArcGIS Server technology, this implies you can assemble a robust framework to utilize web administrations with APDM models.

An APDM model may be the best decision for your association, if:

• ERSI geodatabase technology is as of now set up and utilized

• Relational information honesty can be kept up through application rationale.

• SOA technology is as of now set up

• The flexibility of the information model is essential to your organization

• ArcGIS technology is utilized for spatial mapping.

• Blending an assortment of ESRI-based instruments and outsider applications is significant.

Spatial Data Models

Spatial data models are the strategies through which geographical elements are stored and appeared in PC frameworks. There are various manners by which the data is spoken to in a PC framework. Most importantly, there is map data. Guide data is one of the most straightforward strategies to comprehend fundamental layman's perspectives. This is because it conspicuously exhibits the areas and names of specific territories. This shows lines and geographical focuses that are straightforward.

Alongside guide data, there is likewise characteristic data. It is the sort of data that is unmistakable and will be GIS connected to theoutline. This kind of data is gathered by individual states, regions, and urban areas and can be utilized in registration tracts. Your own specific association's databases will be regularly joined with the databases that are purchased from different sources and means.

Alongside guide data, picture data is another approach to comprehend spatial data in an all the more straightforward way. Picture data can be drawn from satellite pictures and aerial photos. It can likewise be drawn from checked maps, implying that they have been changed over from a printed arrangement to an advanced configuration.

Data models are settled upon guidelines to guarantee that nation lines and region lines not to cover. They are completely basic in choosing what is in a GIS and for supporting GIS programming. Data models fall into two essential classifications: vector and raster.

 Each model has its very own particular advantages. By utilizing vector, it is conceivable to speak to data at its unique goals and structure without speculation. Moreover, the realistic yield from vector frameworks is commonly additionally satisfying to the eye as they utilize conventional cartographic portrayal. As most of the data is in vector structure, there is no requirement for data change. Vector takes into consideration top productivity in the encoding of topology. In any case, the area of every vertex must be stored expressly with vector spatial data. With the goal for it to be best, the majority of the vector data must be changed over into a geological structure. Another disservice of the vector model is that consistent data, for example, height data isn't adequately spoken to in vector structure.

The master model has a few favorable circumstances and hindrances too. Raster is useful to clients because of how the data is stored, the appropriate examination procedure is commonly simple to break down and perform. Raster maps are helpful for numerical demonstrating and quantitative examination. Likewise, because actor maps chip away at lattice frameworks, they are entirely good with raster-based reappropriate administrations. Despite the majority of the advantages of a master model, there are likewise disservices. Since it is a cell framework, the extent of the cell is the thing that decides the goals at which the majority of the data is exhibited. What's more, if there are large amounts of data to process, that raster framework can make the assignment somewhat repetitive because they typically reflect one specific trademark for a territory.

How to Become a Data Scientist

A QUICK REFRESHER

When you are millennial on the chase for another activity or you as of now have a vocation that you have to kick off, Big Data is your best expectation. Why Big Data? In the present propelled period where everything is being done through PC, large measures of data are put away as ones. 7.6 billion individuals on the planet utilize the web out of close to home or expert need so the ratio of data created will be a pervasive amount. People are fit for filtering through just such a significant amount of data before the constant stream of data overpowers our psyches. In any case, in our minds, we have the way to comprehend all difficulties imaginable through some snappy utilization of compound scientific thoughts and some essential PC applications. Massive data is tied in with breaking down extensive data sets to uncover examples and patterns, mainly as they identify with human conduct and associations.

What's in store

This period has seen a lot of modernization, and with PCs being used in each field, there has been an exponential increment in the measure of data we create. What that implies for you is that there will be a lot of chances to thrive as a data researcher or a data investigator.

Accreditation IS A MUST

Like each other aspect of life, affirmation assumes a critical job. Accomplishing an endorsement from a reputable source not just tells your manager that you are knowledgeable about the topic, it additionally discloses to them that you are devoted and will go the additional mile to improve your insight.

HOW CERTIFICATION CAN BENEFIT YOU

A decent affirmation program will dependably ensure you are altogether prepared in the essential and propelled parts of the field. Courses are accessible in both online and disconnected variants as indicated by the comfort for the competitors. For individuals who like learning at their very own pace, online adaptation comes profoundly suggested. Individuals who lean toward a very close homeroom condition for their training can generally choose the disconnected form of the confirmation program.

Contrasts BETWEEN OFFLINE AND ONLINE

The nature of the substance that will be instructed to the hopefuls won't contrast, as indicated by the strategy for the introduction. Individuals who decide on the online mode will be educated through a progression of prerecorded video addresses by probably the most qualified people in their fields. The online session will be loaded up with intuitive tests to strengthen what the hopeful has realized. The study hall rendition, then again, will have increasingly intuitive sessions where they can bring up their issue and find a solution on the spot. The individuals who settle on the online course will have an approach to suggest conversation starters online for the educators and will have the chance to examine subjects with other similarly invested individuals that will empower them to thrive.

YOUR NEXT STEP

Diligent work and devotion are an unquestionable requirement for a prospering vocation. As somebody who effectively needs to seek after his or her fantasy, frequently picking the correct establishment from which to get your authentication turns into the most significant situation of all.

Why Become a Data Scientist?

Why you scored less on a test? Reasons can be many like; you were not well, had no notes, didn't get ample opportunity to amend, got occupied by some different issues, and so on. These are bits of knowledge, and they originated from activity data you have signed in your mind. This is data science in its most comfortable structure.

DATA SCIENCE AND ITS USES

Data science bargains in essential measures of data. It is gathered from a few inner and outer sources like activity, preferences, audio, recordings, messages, and pictures, and so forth is unstructured and crude. One has to scourge through it and find significant experiences which will help in essential leadership and foresee the future needs of the business or business.

So almost certainly that data science is of real use in different businesses like innovation, therapeutic, amusement, retail and discount, money, producing and so on. There are a few uses of data science in these ventures like:

• Creation and advancement of web crawlers, to make them quicker and productive.

• I am making calculations for voice acknowledgment, which empowers a client to give orders with no physical versatility.

• Face and picture acknowledgment programming utilized via web-based networking media platforms and even cell phones for security reasons.

• You are making better suggestion calculations for different sites and portable applications, which monitors your preferences and allude in like manner.

• I am giving better gaming encounters.

• Utilized for credit chance recognition and averting misrepresentation and robberies.

DATA SCIENTISTS AND THEIR ROLE

The individuals who are in charge of breaking down data just as finding key answers for a business concern ought to have a range of abilities of a mathematician, analyst, examiner, and PC software engineer. They ought to have the astuteness for business correspondence and administration too because data researchers ought to likewise have the option to comprehend the data experiences and use it profitably.

Exercises performed by data researchers:

• Lead investigate and pose inquiries.

• Gather data.

• Store and gathering data.

• Perfect and scour data.

• Break down and investigate the data.

• Make calculations utilizing inductions and destinations.

• Clarify the outcomes.

• Suggest necessary and useful changes.

HOW TO BE A DATA SCIENTIST?

Above all else, the prerequisite is interest and curiosity to pose inquiries that were never asked, to look for problems and their answers. Other than that, different specialized and scholarly viewpoints are to be secured as well:

• Arithmetic.

• Measurements.

• Programming abilities like calculations and data structures.

• Data mining

• Data cleaning

• Data are detailing methods.

• Python, R, SAS dialects.

• SQL databases, C/C++, Java

• Data blurring like with Amazon S3.

• Platforms like Hadoop, Apache Flink, Apache Spark, and so on.

One ought to have business abilities as well, as viable correspondence, critical thinking, logical data investigation, industry learning.

There are a few choices in the field of data science like you can be engineer, Architect, stage designer (Apache engineer). Organizations of each size are wandering in data science, so one thing is distinct that the interest for such researchers will stay high.

Chapter 8: Visualization and Results

So far we've discussed the theoretical and technical aspects of data science and machine learning, but there is one more addition to your skillset that needs to be addressed, and that's visualization. Creating visualizations with Python is vital for any aspiring data scientist because it can easily enrich a project and communicate information a lot more clearly and efficiently.

Visualization involves the use of plots, graphics, tables, interactive charts, and much more. Viewing data through an artistic representation helps users greatly in analyzing it because, let's face it, looking at colorful charts makes things clearer than endless strings of numbers that tire your eyes. Visualization helps with operations that involve data comparisons, complex measurements, or identifying patterns.

In this chapter, we are going to briefly discuss the basics of visualization and explore tools such as matplotlib and bokeh. Knowing how to efficiently communicate information to others is a crucial skill, and even though you are only at the beginning of your journey, you should get an idea of the concepts and tools behind visualization.

Matplotlib

Since visualization is a complex topic that requires its own book, we are going to stick to the basics of using Python to create various graphic charts. We are going to go through some examples with code that will serve as the building blocks of visualization examples.

So what is matplotlib? It is basically a Python package that is designed for plotting graphics. It was created because there was little to no integration between the programming language and other tools designed specifically for graphical representations. If you already became familiar with

MATLAB, you might notice that the syntax is very similar. That's because this package was heavily influenced by MATLAB and the module we are going to focus on is fully compatible with it. The "matplotlib.pyplot" module will be the core of this basic introduction to visualization.

Creating, improving, and enriching your graphical representation is easy with plypot commands, because with this module you can make changes to instantiated figures. Now let's go through some examples and discuss the basic guidelines that will allow you to create your own visualization draft.

First, you need to import all the modules and packages by typing the following lines in Python:

In: import numpy as np

import matplotlib.pyplot as plt

import matplotlib as mpl

Now let's start by first drawing a function. This is the most basic visualization, as it requires only a series of x coordinates that are mapped on the y axis. This is known as a *curve representation* because the results are stored in two vectors. Keep in mind that the precision of the visual representation depends on the number of mapping points. The more we have, the higher the precision, so let's take an example with 50 points.

In: import numpy as np

import matplotlib.pyplot as plt

x = np.linspace(0, 5, 50)

y_cos = np.cos(x)

y_sin = np.sin(x)

Next, we are going to map the y axis to the sine and cosine functions with the help of 50 numbers from 0 to 5 that are at an equal distance from each other. This is how the code looks:

```
In: plt.figure() # we start by initializing a figure

plt.plot(x,y_cos) # next we plot a series of coordinates as a line

plt.plot(x,y_sin)

plt.xlabel('x') # this labels the x axis

plt.ylabel('y') # this labels the y axis

plt.title('title') # we add a title

plt.show() # and close the figure
```

The result should be a visualization of curve plotting.

We can also use multiple panels to better visualize the two curves on separate panels. Type in the following code:

```
In: import matplotlib.pyplot as plt

In: plt.subplot(1,2,1) # the parameters define 1 row, 2 columns, and activation

plt.plot(x,y_cos,'r--')

plt.title('cos')

plt.subplot(1,2,2)

plt.plot(x,y_sin,'b-')

plt.title('sin')

plt.show()
```

As a result, you should now see a display of the sine and cosine curves on two separate panels.

But what if we want to visualize our data by using a histogram? Histograms are one of the best visualization methods when we want to clearly see how variables are distributed. Let's create an example where we have two distributions with standard deviation. One of them will have an average of 0, and the other 3.

In: import numpy as np

import matplotlib.pyplot as plt

x = np.random.normal(loc=0.0, scale=1.0, size=500)

z = np.random.normal(loc=3.0, scale=1.0, size=500)

plt.hist(np.column_stack((x,z)), bins=20, histtype='bar',

color = ['c','b'], stacked=True)

plt.grid()

plt.show()

Interactive Visualization

Interactive visualization that is processed inside a browser became very popular due to the success of D3.js, which is a JavaScript library used for creating web-based data visualization with interactive features. This tool is preferred over other methods because there is no latency, meaning data is delivered fast, and visualization can be personalized in many ways.

For Python, we have a similar tool to D3.js called Bokeh (a Japanese term used in photography). This can be found as a component of the pydata stack and is fully interactive, customizable, and efficient. Its purpose is to simplify the creation of visual representation methods that are otherwise complex and time consuming for the data scientist. With Bokeh, you can create interactive plots, dashboards, charts, and other visual representations that can handle even large data sets.

For the purposes of this book, we are going to discuss this topic only briefly and focus on matplotlib-based plots. Feel free to explore this tool on your own, because it is intuitively designed with the user in mind and the documentation for it is plentiful. Let's start by first installing this tool with the following command:

pip install bokeh

Now let's get ready to put it to the test with the following code:

In: import numpy as np

from bokeh.plotting import figure, output_file, show

x = np.linspace(0, 5, 50)

y_cos = np.cos(x)

output_file("cosine.html")

p = figure()

p.line(x, y_cos, line_width=2)

show(p)

Let's explain how this code works. We create an html file and upload it to the browser. If you used Jupyter until this point, keep in mind that this kind of interactive visualization won't work with it due to our output preference, which is the output_file. Now you can use any website to incorporate the output. Next, you will notice that there are various tools on the right side of the plot. These tools allow you to personalize the chart by enlarging it, and manipulating it with dragging and scrolling. Bokeh is an interactive tool that can be integrated with other packages as well. If you become familiar with tools such as Seaborn or ggplot, you can transfer the visual representation from them into Bokeh. The method used to achieve this is "to_bokeh" and it simply ports charts from other visualization tools. You can also use pandas functions together with Bokeh, such as data conversions.

Chapter 9: Most Common Data science Problems:

Regardless of whether you pursue a full-time job in the field, or if you're using data analytics in your pre-existing career, you'll face certain problems with your work. You can't always have a flawless and efficient workflow, no-one can, if you could you'd soon enough become obsolete because there'd be countless people like you.

While some parts of working in data science are utterly amazing, there are still some issues. You can easily get frustrated, especially since most of your superiors won't know in detail what is it you do. It's very difficult to communicate to non-data-analysts precisely what you do. Because of this, the post is prone to misunderstandings and mismanagement.

While all that's true, some of the problems you'll have can be managed and resolved. In this section, we'll look at the most common complaints that people working with data analytics have had in the past, as well as how to resolve them without much consequence.

1. Management Expects The World

This issue is especially prevalent in positions which require you to do a degree of data modeling. Most of data modeling concerns gathering and cleaning the data so that it's actually usable. This is obviously quite a bit of an issue on the manager's fault, as many of them will just suddenly come up with an idea and expect it to be done last-minute.

Obviously, sometimes the modelers are at fault, but unfortunately, more often than not it's managers simply not understanding the job. In the management world, it's quite common to insert things last-minute, but in data analytics that's basically impossible.

Your manager might just pop in and say "Hey, we're gonna include a social media history in our latest analysis. Cool? Cool, I'll see you in 15 minutes when it's done."

Now, if you sigh at this kind of request, then at least there are some solutions for it. Not resolving this issue is bound to either cause serious delays, or some serious dissatisfaction from your managers. The worst thing here is that both sides of the argument are entirely understandable. The data scientists simply can't deal with this in such a short timespan, and managers will have a hard time understanding that.

 Serious complaints about managers being unreasonable and expecting the world are quite common in most technical fields, especially those concerning programming and AI. Fortunately, some solutions exist, and most of them are concerned with improving your communication skills, while at the same time being clear about the possibilities of what is possible, and what isn't.

Let's run through some solutions now.

First of all, you should keep communication open, but keep a firm "no changes" date. After that date, make sure your manager is aware no changes will be processed. Unfortunately, some managers will not be swayed by this.

Be clear about what you can or cannot do. You can't expect your manager to be perfectly well versed in data analytics. The main mistake managers make here is expecting data scientists to utilize datasets which either contain bad, little, or no data and actually have something to show for it at the end of the day.

It's imperative to explain to your manager what you can and cannot do. Give them a few useful articles to read about what ML and AI can actually accomplish, rather than what they've probably read. These days ML and

AI are being hyped up to be essentially omnipotent, and capable of turning any dataset into extremely valuable information.

Unfortunately, as you know, this is quite far from the truth. The analysis you make has a limit on how good it can be, and that limit is the quality of the data you're given. Naturally, you can use interpolation and extrapolation to "plug" the holes in a dataset, but it's not like there's a magic wand you can just point at the computer to create data. If you're given a week of sales info, it doesn't matter how good you are; you won't be able to accurately predict the sales of next year.

The best thing you can do about this is to pay attention to what kind of company you apply to. Do they already have many data scientists on board? Do they collect a lot of good data already? Are they maybe adaptable enough to start collecting it as soon as you join? If the answer to these questions is no, you might want to reconsider working there. It's important to address this early on so it doesn't affect you in the future.

Besides that, try to explain to your manager that last-minute alterations are very difficult, and try to use phrases like "Yes, I could totally do that, it's just going to add about 5 days to the schedule." Your manager's going to be singing a different tune soon.

Misunderstanding How Data Works

Generally, people think of data as a set of information, a truth if you will. This couldn't be farther from the truth. Data is merely facts until someone comes by and puts some context into it.

This is an issue that can affect basically everyone; your boss, your manager, even you might fall into this faulty mindset. Being careful not to think about data as the information is one of the most crucial parts of being a data analytics expert.

Fundamentally, it's extremely important to remember that even if your title is "data analyst" when it comes to actual work, the analyst comes before the data. Fostering a data-first culture in the workplace is a surefire way to have every one of your endeavors heralded by utter failure. It's easy to forget that data needs context to be useful, and it is so, so easy to fall down the slippery slope of worshiping data.

Giving the context is your job; your job is to think about the data, to frame it. The data itself is like a wench is to a mechanic. You don't go praising the wench for fixing the car, so you shouldn't rely on the data too much either. You need to know the broader conditions, for example, market trends which aren't in the data need to be considered.

While your managers might be most inclined to trust in the numbers, your job is to reveal where those numbers might be faulty, what might be affecting them, and what the truth is closest to. Fortunately, this is an easy problem to solve; just let them have it.

If your manager gets burned for a few million because they trusted data more than you, then next time you can be sure that they're going to pay more attention to your words next time around.

Now, you also need to consider the bias of data collection when dealing with work. All data collection processes are susceptible to certain biases. Let's say that you're analyzing a market based on how many people buy from the company site. In this case, the bias is on younger, more tech-savvy people, as older people are more likely to buy from brick and mortar stores.

Taking The Blame For Bad News

Unfortunately, when it comes to being a data scientist, your recommendations are likely to end up in one of three ways: A bonus, a promotion, or expulsion from work.

The danger of working as anyone that concerns themselves with data analytics is that you will often have to profess the bad news to your bosses. Unfortunately, not all of them have read Sun Tzu's book of war and refuse to shoot the messenger. If your data analysis shows that there are serious problems in the company, or even that the company is headed towards its own destruction, it's quite likely your bosses will be less than kind.

Presenting this information can feel very awkward and uncomfortable, and can sometimes end up in disastrous consequences. In most cases, you won't be to blame for this, but you are an easy link to scapegoat. Any manager can easily put the blame on you, and your boss might not be well versed enough to see through it.

Now, ultimately, this is an issue you cannot precisely solve. If your boss is blaming you for what you find out after digging through the company data, you'll probably want to check if your resume is up to date as soon as possible. You don't need, and shouldn't put up with being attacked for doing your job. If you're really committed to solving the issue, try assigning blame to yourself. You can't hold your job if you sidestep telling your boss about things that were others' responsibilities.

Even if companies are trying to be modern and adapt to changes in the industry swiftly, fundamentally, most companies are still run in an old-fashioned manner. The complaint Strand has expressed is extremely common in data scientists, and the chances that you aren't going to run into an example of this in your career are close to nil. A recent study has shown that ⅔ of all managers distrust data, and would rather hand over decision making onto their intuition, rather than trusting scientists.

Unfortunately, these are generally mid-level managers, who have just enough power to feel like they're important, but not enough power to affect the decisions made on a broader, company-wide scale. Most data scientists get stuck with working for one of these at least at one point in their career.

You'll find that you have to convince the management of practically every new decision you have to do. Do you need better data collection? Are you trying to make a financial model of the company spending so you can budget accordingly? Well too bad, because Steve from management has decided that his intuition tops that. Even in the case that you've actually gotten approval for your project, you'll still face challenges with getting management to well...act accordingly. Even if your model showed that your company spends too much on marketing, good luck convincing your managers of that.

This is why skills in communications are so useful for any role related to data science. All of the analytical skills in the world are going to be useless if there's nobody to take action upon them. Your results won't have even the slightest impact on the firm unless you're able to engage upper management enough with your speech, data presentation, etc. This is why it's important to keep in mind soft skills, as well as your ability to do presentations and visualizations of projects. It's much easier to convince management if you're showing them shapes and figures, rather than Excel spreadsheets. Try running your presentation by a friend that has absolutely no technical skills; this will prove to you whether your presentation is fine. Pay attention to what questions are posed to you, and try to address them more clearly in the presentation.

It's also sometimes useful to try to explain your ideas to an inanimate object. This lets you pay attention to how you talk, as well as how you communicate the data without the need to have an actual person with you there.

With that being said, don't feel too bad if it doesn't work out. Sometimes your managers will simply elect not to listen to the data, or decide that something is simply more important. A relatively recent case of this was when data analytics showed that Grace & Frankie's promotional images worked the best without the show's star. The team of executives at Netflix then had to think about the pros and cons of excluding the lead, Jane Fonda, from the images.

In the end, they elected not to, partly not to anger the lead, and partly because the show would be more "iconic" if the lead was present, rather than if promotional images were used exclusively as an advertisement.

The only fortunate thing here is that this is a bit of a cascading issue. If you fail a few times, management is unlikely to ever trust you again. On the other hand, if you bring success a few times, you'll build their confidence in your data, and they'll be much more likely to trust you with important projects. It is a matter of picking your battles, so to speak, try to only engage where you are absolutely sure you can succeed.

Communication As A Solution

You might have noticed that the overarching theme here is communication, and it is. While your data analytics and portfolio are the things that will let you get the job and perform it well, mere performance isn't enough. To make your day to day life better, and your career more successful, you have to practice communication and learn how to speak to your managers in the most effective ways possible.

If you're looking to hone your communication skills, look no further than those same managers you take issue with. They tend to be quite good at communicating with their bosses, talking to them, and paying attention to the terms and tactics they use can be an excellent way to learn communication skills.

Above all, it is important to practice. Try to make your every email sound more professional, your every message to be more concise and effective. The same way you analyze in your job, analyze your approach to your job, think about what the most effective words to use are, and when to use them.

Chapter 10: Linear Classifiers

As you go through and work with some machine learning, especially when it comes to supervised learning, you may find that two of the most common tasks that are going to be required here will include both the linear regression and the linear classifier. The linear regression is helpful in some situations because it can predict the value of your data—then, the linear classifier is useful because it focuses on the class. While both of these are useful in machine learning, we are going to look at the linear classifier and some of the steps that you will use when you bring this up in machine learning.

You will find out quickly that when you are working on machine learning, these classification problems are very prevalent, and they will take up a minimum of 80 percent of the tasks that you will do in machine learning. Classification aims to predict how probable it is that each class is going to happen given the inputs that you decide to put in, the label (the label is going to be the dependent variables here), and the class.

If your dependent variable or the label only comes in with two classes to work within the beginning, then you know that the algorithm that you are working with is a binary classifier. If you would like to work with a classifier that has more than one class, this means that it will be able to tackle any of the labels with three or more classes.

Let's look at an example of this one. Many of the classification problems that are also considered binary can predict how likely it is that your customer will come back, after making one purchase, and purchase again. But if you would like the system to predict the animal that you have placed into an image, you will instead work with a classification problem that is known as multiclass. This is because there will be more than two types of animals that can show up in the picture.

Measuring Your Linear Classifier Performance

Now, we need to take a look at the linear classifier a bit more and how you can measure how well it can perform. Accuracy is essential with any of the learning algorithms that you work with, and it is one of the best places to start. The performance overall of this classifier is going to be measured using the metric of accuracy—this is how important it is for you.

When we talk about accuracy, it is the measurement of whether the algorithm can collect the proper values that you have, and then it can divide that number by the total number of observations that are present. Looking at an example of this, if you have an accuracy value that is set at 85 percent, this means that your algorithm is going to be right 85 percent of the time, but then it is going to be wrong the other 15 percent. Of course, if you are working with numbers and data, you want to make sure that the accuracy is as high as possible.

As you take a look at the accuracy, you should also note that there is a shortcoming with this metric, and this is never more apparent than when you are looking at a class of imbalance. A set of data that ends up not being balanced is going to occur when the number of observations that show up isn't equal in all of the groups that you have.

To understand this, let's say that you are doing a classification challenge of a rare event with the function of logistics. You would need to think about the classifier that you would like to use, and that will include estimating how many patients died when they were in contact with a disease. In the data, you see that five percent of the infected patients were going to die.

From this information, you would be able to train your chosen classifier to make sure that it can predict the number of deaths is going to occur for those with the disease. Then you can go through and use the metric of accuracy to evaluate how that clinic or hospital is performing. With this example, the classifier can go and look at the information. Maybe it predicts that there are going to be no deaths for the set of data as a whole. This is going to be accurate about 95 percent of the time, which gives it some margin of error.

The next thing that we need to focus on here is something known as the confusion matrix. This is going to be a better way to take a look at how well the classifier can perform compared to the accuracy that you were able to do above. When you decide to bring in the confusion matrix, you will be able to get a visual about how accurate the classifier is by comparing the actual and the predicted classes. The binary confusion matrix is going to consist of squares. If you decide to work with this kind of confusion matrix, there are a few different parts that come with it including

1. TP: This is going to be known as the true positive. This is going to contain all of the predicted values that were predicted correctly as an actual positive.

2. FP: This is going to be the false ones—or the ones that were predicted incorrectly. They were predicted usually as positive, but they were negative. This means that the negative values show up, but they had been predicted ahead of time as positive.

3. FN: This is a false negative. This is when your positive values are predicted as negative.

4. TN: this is going to be the true negative. These are the values that were predicted correctly and predicted as actual negative.

When a computer programmer takes a look at this confusion matrix to use it, they are going to get a lot of information to use. The confusion matrix can help you get a nice clear look at the predicted class, and the actual class, so that you can compare and contrast what is going on with the data that you have.

Are Sensitivity and Precision Important?

The confusion matrix is one of the best things that you can work with when it comes to looking through the linear classification and understanding the information that is in your data. But when you do this kind of matrix, you will find that a lot of information will come your way. These matrices are also going to give you some insights when it comes to a true positive and a false positive in the information that you have. However, even though this is a great thing to work with, there are still some cases when it would be better to go with a more concise metric to help you understand the information at hand.

The first thing that we need to look at here with the metric that you use is precision. The precision metric is important because it shows us how accurate the positive class is going to be. This may sound confusing, but it means that this precision metric is going to provide you a measure of how likely the positive class prediction is going to be correct in the long run. To do this, you can use the formula below to make this easier:

Precision = TP / (TP + FP)

The maximum amount, or score, that you are going to end up with here is one. And this is going to show up the classifier and be correct when you have a positive value. While precision, and knowing how precise the metric is ahead of time can be super critical to the success that you get, it is not going to be all that you need to look for, mainly because it can ignore the negative class. This metric is something that you would be able to use, but it is more helpful if you pair it up with what is known as the recall metric. The recall is also going to be known as the true positive rate, or the sensitivity rate.

From this point, we also need to have a good idea of the sensitivity that comes with this learning algorithm. This sensitivity can be important because it will let you know the ratio of positive classes that your algorithm can figure out correctly. The metric is a good way to model and take a look at a positive formula that will help you work with this algorithm and figure out its sensitivity will include the following:

Recall = TP / (TP + FN)

Using TensorFlow and Linear Classifiers Together

Now, we are going to take a look at this idea and discuss some of the ways that you can use this library, especially when it comes to a linear classifier algorithm. The first thing that we are going to be able to do to help combine the two of these is to use a data set that is a census.

The whole aim of doing this is to help us use the variable in a census data set to help us come up with a prediction of the income of those people who are going to participate in this data. Note that the income for this example is going to be known as a binary variable.

For this example, we are going to set the variable that is binary at one of the income of the individual, and it is set to be above $50,000. However, if the income ends up being under this dollar amount, then we will need to write out the variable that is binary as 0. The data set that we can work with to make this all happen can be written out in eight variables that are categorical and include the following:

- Native country

- Sex

- Race

- Relationship

- Occupation

- Marital status

- Education

- Place of work

And on top of this, we are going to take a look in this at six of the continuous variables. These are going to include:

- *HOURS_WEEK*
- *CAPITAL_LOSS*
- *CAPITAL_GAIN*
- *EDUCATION_NUM*
- *FNLWGT*
- *AGE*

Once we have this information, you can open up the TensorFlow library to figure out what the probability is. This probability is going to help us figure out which customers can fit into each group (which ones make more than $50,000 and which ones earn less than $50,000).

In this example, you are going to separate each of your customers into two groups. The first group will be the individuals who listed themselves as making more than $50,000. And the second group is going to be individuals who will make under $50,000. When the individuals are separated into these two groups, you will then be able to look more at their background information, and figure out some information about them like their race, sex, where they work, where they live, and anything else that you would like about them. This can provide some valuable insights for a business to learn more about their customers and how they may purchase things in the future.

Many businesses like to do this because it allows them to learn more about their customers, and ensures that they can figure out who to advertise too. It can also be useful when it comes to customers who come back and make purchases more than once. The business would be able to use this information to figure out how likely it is that a first-time customer is going to come back, and can change up their marketing and advertising to reach these kinds of people more often.

Discriminative Models and Generative Models

At some point, you will need to create some parameters that go with your linear classifier. And when it is time to work with these parameters, two classes or methods can help you with this. These are pretty broad, and they are known as either the generative model or the discriminative model.

Methods that come with the generative model are going to be functions that look at the conditional density. The examples of these types of algorithms that you may use with machine learning will include the Linear Discriminant Analysis, which will assume the Gaussian conditional density models, or you can work with the classifier that relies on the Naïve Bayes algorithm.

The other method that we brought up above is going to be the discriminative model. These are going to be vital because they are going to work to make sure that any output that you get from the program is as high in quality as it can be, especially when you work with the training set. It is possible that when you are doing with the training that you will need to add in some additional terms, but they can cost more and may be able to perform the regularization of the final model that you get. There are a few options that the computer programmer can choose from when they work with discriminative training, and these options will include:

1. Logistic regression: This one is important because it can show us the likelihood estimation of linear classifiers. It is going to do this with the assumption that the observed training set is going to be generated through a binomial model and it is going to depend on the kind of output that the classifier provides to us.

2. Perception: This is a type of algorithm that you would like to use in some of your machine learning because you will use it to fix up any errors that may occur in your training set, which makes it more accurate overall.

3. Support vector machine Remember this one from before? It can work with your discrimination model as well. This is going to be the type of algorithm that you will be able to use and maximize quite a bit. You can use examples that can hose up in the hyperplane of the decision and in the training set to help with accuracy.

Despite the name that comes with it, the LDA is not going to be one of the options that come with the discriminative models, at least in this method. However, the name is going to make sense if you can compare it to the other algorithms that fit into this model. You will find that this LDA algorithm can fit more in with the supervised machine learning method, and it will instead be there to work on the labels of your data. But then the PCA will be more of an unsupervised machine learning algorithm, and it will go through and, on purpose, ignore all of the labels that you have present there.

In many cases, you will be able to work with discriminative training, but as you do, you will be able to get an accuracy that is much higher compared to the conditional density functions. But, if you do work with those later models, handling the data that is missing in that set is going to be easier. So, as you can see, you have to give and take a bit here. You have to pick whether you want a better accuracy in your information, or if you are going to want to handle some of the missing points, and go from there.

Chapter 11: Setting Up PyCharm

Writing scripts in the text editor is only going to allow you to do so much and eventually, you'll find yourself needing something a little more powerful in order to edit your work and try it on the fly. This will also allow you to view your game assets and all the files in your project and much more.

To get started, head over to the JetBrains website (www.jetbrains.com) and then download PyCharm using the link on the main page. This will then download automatically. Choose the Community version in order to get the free and basic version that will take up the least space on your computer.

Installation is super easy: just click on the .exe you've downloaded and then set a folder to install the files to. With that done, it should execute on its own and install everything for you.

Finding Your Way Around the IDE

Once that is up and running, you can simply click on the icon in your Start Menu in order to launch the IDE. Select 'New Project' and then choose the location for that project on your computer, as well as the name of the program you're going to make. For now, you can type anything in here!

Project Window

With that done, the IDE will now boot up. So what exactly are you looking at here?

What you should see, is three separate windows on your screen. On the left is your 'Project' window. This window shows you the project files, which will include any code, as well as any libraries you use and also things like graphics, sounds and more. If you right click on the project folder up at the top, then you'll find that you can create a new file, including a new 'Python File'. This of course is a file that contains script that you'll be writing, so do that right now and you'll now have somewhere that you can start writing! Call it whatever you like.)

If you want to, you can right click on the project window and select 'SHOW IN EXPLORER'. This will open up the folder in Windows Explorer, thereby allowing you to view and edit the files as you would any other.

Below the main folder (and now you're new file), you should find that there is another folder called 'External Libraries'. Therefore, these are external packages of code that provide you with modules you can use in your own programs. We'll see in future how you can use and install these additional libraries as you go.

Something useful you can see right now though, that will actually help you to get a better understanding of how all this works, is the Python Standard Library modules. And we actually went ahead and used the library 'Random' in order to generate our random number? Well, if you click on the External Libraries folder, then on Python 3.6.0 (or whichever version you have installed) and then on 'Lib', you'll be able to see a large list of folders and .py files. These are our modules and libraries!

And if you scroll down the list, then you can actually see 'Random' right there – as well as 'Turtle'. If you click on one, you'll find it opens in another tab next to the blank script you've made! Don't edit these (or you'll risk damaging their functionality) but if you want to learn how to use different libraries, then looking through their code to find the different modules within can give you some idea.

On the whole though, this is some pretty high-end stuff… so let's just close that for now!

Script Window

On the right hand side, you will find that you have your empty code page (now that you've created it in the project). This is where you code and it should look a little similar to the editor we've been using through IDLE.

Something *new* though that you may not notice right away, is that our script window will show us our errors by underlining them in red. So if you type:

Print "You WIN!!!"

And you're using Python 3, then you will see that the space is underlined red. This tells you that there's something wrong with your code and you can that way edit it if you need to!

If you hold the mouse over the red wiggly line, it will even tell you something about the problem. In this case, it says 'End of statement expected'. Fix it and the red line will go away.

Another cool thing about coding here, is that you can see at a glance where all of the errors are located throughout your code. Look at the scrollbar on the right and you'll see a selection of yellow and red lines (if you have a lot of code here). Click on any of those lines and your code will jump *straight* to the line where there's a problem.

If you do have a lot of code, then you'll notice that *some* of the lines aren't red but are rather yellow. These yellow lines are areas where your code isn't *wong* per-say but could maybe be better. For example, it might be that a line isn't actually doing anything helpful. If you just write:

Print

Then there is no rule that you can't do this but it isn't actually doing anything useful. Thus, it is highlighted in yellow and if you hover the mouse over it, it will say 'Statement seems to have no effect and can be replaced with a function call to have effect.'

Finally, you might also notice that there are some blue lines down the side when you have lots of code in this window. These blue lines change position depending on what you have clicked on and the great thing about this, is that it lets you find instances of the same words.

Why might this be useful? Well for instance, if you were looking for instances of a particular variable that you created, then you could find it just once, click on it and then see where else you have used it in your code.

You can also use this in conjunction with comments to create little bookmarks throughout your code. For example, you could keep a list of modules at the top of your code as comments, then click on one to quickly jump to it when you need to.

Another neat feature is the ability to expand and compress loops and modules by clicking on the small 'plus' and 'minus' figures next to them. This can shorten your code considerably for the sake of quickly and easily flicking through.

In short, using an IDE like PyCharm will save you time by providing more powerful formatting and editing tools.

Game Window

Our final and most exciting window though is the one down the bottom called 'Run Game'. Can you guess what this does yet? Type your code into the script view and then click the green 'Play' button on the left of the Game window at any time and it will run. You can then click on it to interact with it as you normally would and this will save you a lot of time and effort versus having to save your program and run it separately every time – especially if you have multiple different .py files all working together for a single, larger project.

If this window isn't here when you first boot up PyCharm, then don't worry. You should be able to open it by heading to Run > Run 'Game'.

Note that this window will occasionally act differently, as will the main scripting console.

```
from turtle import *

color('red', 'yellow')

begin_fill()

while True:

    forward(200)

    left(170)

    if abs(pos()) < 1:

        break

end_fill()

done()
```

Now, if you click play, you'll find that a new window breaks out of the one you're currently in and plays the demo.

So What is an IDE?

Note that an IDE is only an interface. At first, it can be all too easy to confuse an IDE with the programming language itself. But remember:

you already installed Python onto your PC and this came afterward. This is simply a tool for *interacting* with Python and for giving you everything all in one place. It is an 'integrated development environment'.

To demonstrate this, whether you use *raw_input* or *input*, will not be dependent on the IDE but rather on the version of Python that you installed. And likewise, the same is true for *Print ""* or *Print("")*.

This is why 'PyCharm' makes so much sense – it is charming the snake!

This also means that you can use any one of numerous different IDEs and find the one that suits you best. Don't worry though, although we've only discussed the one, you will find that they are largely much of a muchness with the same basic windows and functionality. You can use any IDE you like but just bear in mind that it will be a little easier going forward if you are using the same interface as I will be. For its simplicity and free nature, I recommend PyCharm!

Chapter 12: Data frames

A Pandas data frame is just an ordered collection of Pandas series with a common/shared index. At its basic form, a data frame looks more like an excel sheet with rows, columns, labels and headers. To create a data frame, the following syntax is used:

pd.DataFrame(data=None, index=None, columns=None, dtype=None, copy=False)

Usually, the data input is an array of values (of whatever datatype). The index and column parameters are usually lists/vectors of either numeric or string type.

If a Pandas series is passed to a data frame object, the index automatically becomes the columns, and the data points are assigned accordingly.

Example 71: Creating a data frame

In []: df = pd.DataFrame([pool1])   *# passing a series*

df   *# show*

two series

index = 'WWI WWII'.split()

new_df = pd.DataFrame([pool1,pool3],index)
new_df   *# show*

Output:

USA	Britain	France	Germany	
0	1	2	3	4

	USA	Britain	France	Germany
WWI	1	2	3	4
WWII	5	1	3	4

Notice how the first data frame assigns the series labels as column headers, and since no index was assigned, a value of '0' was set at that index i.e. row header.

For the second data frame, the row labels were specified by passing a list of strings ['WWI','WWII'].

Tip: The .split() string method is a quick way of creating lists of strings. It works by splitting a string into its component characters, depending on the delimiter passed to the string method.

For example, let us split this email 'pythonguy@gmail.com' into a list containing the username and the domain name.

```
In []:  # Illustrating the split() method
email = 'pythonguy@gmail.com'
string_vec = email.split('@')
string_vec    # show
A = string_vec[0]; B = string_vec[1] # Extracting values
print('Username:',A,'\nDomain name:',B)
Out[]:  ['pythonguy', 'gmail.com']

   Username: pythonguy
   Domain name: gmail.com
```

To create a data frame with an array, we can use the following method:

Creating dataframe with an array

Array = np.arange(1,21).reshape(5,4) # numpy array

row_labels = 'A B C D E'.split()

col_labels = 'odd1 even1 odd2 even2'.split()

Arr_df = pd.DataFrame(Array,row_labels,col_labels)
Arr_df

Output:

	odd1	even1	odd2	even2
A	1	2	3	4
B	5	6	7	8
C	9	10	11	12
D	13	14	15	16
E	17	18	19	20

Notice how this is not unlike how we create spreadsheets in excel. Try playing around with creating data frames.

Exercise: Create a data frame from a 5 × 4 array of uniformly distributed random values. Include your choice row and column names using the .split() method.

Hint: use the rand function to generate your values, and use the reshape method to form an array.

Now that we can conveniently create Data frames, we are going to learn how to index and grab elements off them.

Tip: Things to note about data frames.

- *They are a collection of series (more like a list with Pandas series as its elements).*
- *They are similar to numpy arrays i.e. they are more like n* ✕ *m dimensional matrices, where 'n' are the rows and 'm' are the columns.*

Example 72: Grabbing elements from a data frame.

The easiest elements to grab are the columns. This is because, by default, each column element is a series with the row headers as labels. We can grab them by using a similar method from the series – indexing by name.

In []: # Grab data frame elements

Arr_df['odd1']   # grabbing first column

Out[]: A   1

B   5

C   9

D   13

E   17
Name: odd1, dtype: int32

Pretty easy, right? Notice how the output is like a Pandas series. You can verify this by using the type(Arr_df['odd1']) command.

When more than one column is grabbed, however, it returns a data frame (which makes sense, since a data frame is a collection of at least two series). To grab more than one column, pass the column names to the indexing as a list. This is shown in the example code below:

In []:# Grab two columns
Arr_df[['odd1','even2']] # grabbing first and last columns

Output:

	odd1	even2
A	1	4
B	5	8
C	9	12
D	13	16
E	17	20

To select a specific element, use the double square brackets indexing notation we learned under array indexing. For example, let us select the value 15 from Arr_df.

In []: Arr_df['odd2']['D']
Out[]: 15

You may decide to break the steps into two, if it makes it easier. This method is however preferred as it saves memory from variable allocation. To explain, let us break it down into two steps.

In []: x = Arr_df['odd2']

x

Out[]: A   3

B   7

C   11

D   15

E   19
Name: odd2, dtype: int32

See that the first operation returns a series containing the element '15'. This series can now be indexed to grab 15 using the label 'D'.

In []: x['D']
Out[]: 15

While this approach works, and is preferred by beginners, a better approach is to get comfortable with the first method to save coding time and resources.

To grab rows, a different indexing method is used.

You can use either data_frame_name.loc['row_name'] or data_frame_name.iloc['row_index'].

Let us grab the row E from Arr_df.

In []: print("using .loc['E']")

    Arr_df.loc['E']

    print('\nusing .iloc[4]')

    Arr_df.iloc[4]

     using .loc['E']

Out[]:

    odd1   17

    even1   18

    odd2   19

    even2 20

    Name: E, dtype: int32

     using .iloc[4]

Out[]:

odd1   17

even1   18

odd2   19

even2   20
Name: E, dtype: int32

See, the same result!

You can also use the row indexing method to select single items.

In []: Arr_df.loc['E']['even2']

 # or

 Arr_df.iloc[4]['even2']

Out[]: 20
Out[]: 20

Moving on, we will try to create new columns in a data frame, and also delete a column.

In []: # Let us add two sum columns to Arr_df

Arr_df['Odd sum'] = Arr_df['odd1']+Arr_df['odd2']

Arr_df['Even sum'] = Arr_df['even1']+Arr_df['even2']
Arr_df

Output:

	odd1	even1	odd2	even2	Odd sum	Even sum
A	1	2	3	4	4	6
B	5	6	7	8	12	14
C	9	10	11	12	20	22

D	13	14	15	16	28	30
E	17	18	19	20	36	38

Notice how the new columns are declared. Also, arithmetic operations are possible with each element in the data frame, just like we did with the series.

Exercise: Add an extra column to this data frame. Call it Total Sum, and it should be the addition of Odd sum and Even sum.

To remove a column from a data frame, we use the data_frame_name.drop() method.

Let us remove the insert a new column and then remove it using the .drop() method.

In []: Arr_df['disposable'] = np.zeros(5)   # *new column*
   Arr_df   #*show*

Output:

	odd1	even1	odd2	even2	Odd sum	Even sum	disposable
A	1	2	3	4	4	6	0.0
B	5	6	7	8	12	14	0.0
C	9	10	11	12	20	22	0.0
D	13	14	15	16	28	30	0.0
E	17	18	19	20	36	38	0.0

To remove the unwanted column:

In []: # to remove

Arr_df.drop('disposable',axis=1,inplace=True)
Arr_df

Output:

	odd1	even1	odd2	even2	Odd sum	Even sum
A	1	2	3	4	4	6
B	5	6	7	8	12	14
C	9	10	11	12	20	22
D	13	14	15	16	28	30
E	17	18	19	20	36	38

Notice the 'axis=1' and 'inplace = True' arguments. These are parameters that specify the location to perform the drop i.e. axis (axis = 0 specifies row operation), and intention to broadcast the drop to the original data frame, respectively. If 'inplace= False', the data frame will still contain the dropped column.

Tip: The 'inplace = False' method is used for assigning an array to another variable without including certain columns.

Conditional selection

Similar to how we conditional selection works with NumPy arrays, we can select elements from a data frame that satisfy a Boolean criterion.

You are expected to be familiar with this method, hence, it will be done in one step.

Example 72: Let us grab sections of the data frame 'Arr_df' where the value is > 5.

In []: # Grab elements greater than five
Arr_df[Arr_df>5]
Output:

	odd1	even1	odd2	even2	Odd sum	Even sum
A	NaN	NaN	NaN	NaN	NaN	6
B	NaN	6.0	7.0	8.0	12.0	14
C	9.0	10.0	11.0	12.0	20.0	22
D	13.0	14.0	15.0	16.0	28.0	30
E	17.0	18.0	19.0	20.0	36.0	38

Notice how the instances of values less than 5 are represented with a 'NaN'.

Another way to use this conditional formatting is to format based on column specifications.

You could remove entire rows of data, by specifying a Boolean condition based off a single column. Assuming we want to return the Arr_df data frame without the row 'C'. We can specify a condition to return values where the elements of column 'odd1' are not equal to '9' (since row C contains 9 under column 'odd1').

In []: # removing row C through the first column
Arr_df[Arr_df['odd1']!= 9]

Output:

	odd1	even1	odd2	even2	**Odd sum**	**Even sum**
A	1	2	3	4	4	6
B	5	6	7	8	12	14
D	13	14	15	16	28	30
E	17	18	19	20	36	38

Notice that row 'C' has been filtered out. This can be achieved through a smart conditional statement through any of the columns.

In []: # does the same thing : remove row 'C'

    # Arr_df[Arr_df['even2']!= 12]

In[]: # Let us remove rows D and E through 'even2'
    Arr_df[Arr_df['even2']<= 12]
Output

	odd1	even1	odd2	even2	**Odd sum**	**Even sum**
A	1	2	3	4	4	6
B	5	6	7	8	12	14
C	9	10	11	12	20	22

Exercise: Remove rows C, D, E via the 'Even sum' column. Also, try out other such operations as you may prefer.

To combine conditional selection statements, we can use the 'logical and, i.e. &', and the 'logical or, i.e. |' for nesting multiple conditions. The regular 'and' and 'or' operators would not work in this case as they are used for comparing single elements. Here, we will be comparing a series of elements that evaluates to true or false, and those generic operators find such operations ambiguous.

Example 73: Let us select elements that meet the criteria of being greater than 1 in the first column, and less than 22 in the last column. Remember, the 'and statement' only evaluates to true if both conditions are true.

| In []:Arr_df[(Arr_df['odd1']>1) & (Arr_df['Even sum']<22)]

Output:

	odd1	even1	odd2	even2	Odd sum	Even sum
B	5	6	7	8	12	14

Only the elements in Row 'B' meet this criterion, and were returned in the data frame.

This approach can be expounded upon to create even more powerful data frame filters.

Missing Data

There are instances when the data being imported or generated into pandas is incomplete or have missing data points. In such a case, the likely solution is to remove such values from the dataset, or to fill in new values based on some statistical extrapolation techniques. While we would not be fully exploring statistical measures of extrapolation (you can read up on that from any good statistics textbook), we would be considering the use of the .dropna() and .fillna() methods for removing and filling up missing data points respectively.

To illustrate this, we will create a data frame – to represent imported data with missing values, and then use these two data preparation methods on it.

Example 73: Another way to create a data frame is by using a dictionary. Remember, a python dictionary is somehow similar to a Pandas series in that they have key-value pairs, just as Pandas series are label-value pairs (although this is a simplistic comparison for the sake of conceptualization).

> In []:# First, our dictionary
>
> dico = {'X':[1,2,np.nan],'Y':[4,np.nan,np.nan],'Z':[7,8,9]}
>
> dico #show
>
> # passing the dictionary to a dataframe
>
> row_labels = 'A B C'.split()
>
> df = pd.DataFrame(dico,row_labels)
> df #show

Output:

{'X': [1, 2, nan], 'Y': [4, nan, nan], 'Z': [7, 8, 9]}

	X	Y	Z
A	1.0	4.0	7
B	2.0	NaN	8
C	NaN	NaN	9

Now, let us start off with the .dropna() method. This removes any 'null' or 'nan' values in the data frame it's called off, either column-wise or row-wise, depending on the axis specification and other arguments passed to the method. It has the following default syntax:

```
df.dropna(axis=0, how='any', thresh=None, subset=None, inplace=False)
```

The 'df' above is the data frame name. The default axis is set to zero, which represent row-wise operation. Hence, at default, the method will remove any row containing 'nan' values.

Let us see what happens when we call this method for our data frame.

In []: # this removes 'nan' row-wise
   df.dropna()

Output:	X	Y	Z
A	1.0	4.0	7

Notice that rows B and C contain at least a 'nan' value. Hence, they were removed.

Let us try a column-wise operation by specifying the axis=1.

In []: # this removes 'nan' column-wise
   df.dropna(axis=1)

Output:

	Z
A	7
B	8
C	9

As expected, only the column 'Z' was returned.

Now, in case we want to set a condition for a minimum number of 'non-nan' values/ actual data points required to make the cut (or escape the cut, depending on your perspective), we can use the 'thresh' (short for threshold) parameter to specify this.

Say, we want to remove 'nan' row-wise, but we only want to remove instances where the row had more than one actual data point value. We can set the threshold to 2 as illustrated in the following code:

In []: # drop rows with less than 2 actual values
```
df.dropna(thresh = 2)
```
Output:

	X	Y	Z
A	1.0	4.0	7
B	2.0	NaN	8

Notice how we have filtered out row C, since it contains only one actual value '9'.

Exercise: Filter out columns in the data frame 'df' containing less than 2 actual data points

Next, let us use the .fillna() method to replace the missing values with our extrapolations.

This method has the following syntax:
```
df.fillna(value=None,   method=None,   axis=None,   inplace=False,   limit=None,
          downcast=None, **kwargs)
```

Tip: Reminder, you can always use shift + tab to check the documentation of methods and functions to know their syntax.

Let us go ahead and replace our 'NaN' values with an 'x' marker. We can specify the 'X' as a string, and pass it into the 'value' parameter in .fillna().

In []: # filling up NaNs

df.fillna('X')

Output:	X	Y	Z
A	1	4	7
B	2	X	8
C	X	X	9

While marking missing data with an 'X' is fun, it is sometimes more intuitive (for lack of a better statistical approach), to use the mean of the affected column as a replacement for the missing elements.

Example 74: Filling up missing data.

Let us first use the mean method to fill up column 'X', then based off that simple step, we will use a for loop to automatically fill up missing data in the data frame.

```
In []: # Replacing missing values with mean in column 'X'

df['X'].fillna(value = df['X'].mean())

Out[]: A    1.0

B    2.0

C    1.5
Name: X, dtype: float64
```

Notice that the value of the third element in column 'X' has changed to 1.5. This is the mean of that column. The one line code that accomplished this could have been broken down into multiple line for better understanding. This is shown below:

```
In []:# variables

xcol_var = df['X']
```

xcol_mean = xcol_var.mean() # *or use mean(xcol_var)*

instruction

xcol_var.fillna(value = xcol_mean)

Out[]: A   1.0

B   2.0

C   1.5
Name: X, dtype: float64

Same results, but more coding and more memory use via variable allocation.

Now, let us automate the entire process.

In []: for i in 'X Y Z'.split():   # *loop*

```
df[i].fillna(value = df[i].mean(),inplace=True)
df          # show
```

Output:

	X	Y	Z		X	Y	Z
A	1.0	4.0	7	A	1.0	4.0	7
B	2.0	4.0	8	B	2.0	NaN	8
C	1.5	4.0	9	C	NaN	NaN	9
	New data frame				Old data frame		

While the output only displays the data frame on the left, the original data frame is put here for comparison. Notice the new values replacing the NaNs. For the column 'Y', the mean is 4.0, since that is the only value present.

This is a small operation that can be scaled for preparing and formatting larger datasets in Pandas.

> *Tip:* The other arguments of the .fillna() method can be explored, including the fill methods: for example, forward-fill - which fills the missing value with the previous row/column value based on the value of the limit parameter i.e. if limit = 1, it fills the next 1 row/column with the previous row/column value; also, the back-fill - which does the same as forward-fill, but backwards.

Group-By

This Pandas method, as the name suggests, allows the grouping of related data to perform combined/aggregate operations on them.

Example 75: Creating a data frame of XYZ store sales.

```
In []: # Company XYZ sales information
       # Dictionary containing needed data
data = {'Sales Person':'Sam Charlie Amy Vanessa Carl Sarah'.split(),
       'Product':'Hp Hp Apple Apple Dell Dell'.split(),
       'Sales':[200,120,340,124,243,350]}
print('XYZ sales information\n_____')  # print info.
serial = list(range(1,7))      # row names from 1-6
df = pd.DataFrame(data,serial)   # build data frame
df
```

Output:

XYZ sales information

	Sales Person	Product	Sales
1	Sam	Hp	200
2	Charlie	Hp	120
3	Amy	Apple	340
4	Vanessa	Apple	124
5	Carl	Dell	243
6	Sarah	Dell	350

From our dataset, we can observe some common items under the product column. This is an example of an entry point for the group-by method in a data set. We can find information about the sales using the product grouping.

In []: # finding sales information by product

```
print('Total items sold: by product')
df.groupby('Product').sum()
```

Total items sold: by product

	Sales
Product	
Apple	464
Dell	593
Hp	320

This is an example of an aggregate operation using groupby. Other functions can be called to display interesting results as well. For example, .count():

```
In []: df.groupby('Product').count()
```

Output:

	Sales Person	Sales
Product		
Apple	2	2
Dell	2	2
Hp	2	2

While the previous operation could not return the 'Sales person' field, since a numeric operation like 'sum' cannot be performed on a string, the count method returns the instances of each product within both categories. Via this output, we can easily infer that XYZ company assigns two salespersons per product, and that each of the sales persons made a sale of the products. However, unlike the sum method, this count method does not give a clearer overview of the sales. This is why so many methods are usually called to explain certain aspects of data. A very useful method for checking multiple information at a time is the .describe() method.

In []: #Getting better info using describe ()
```
df.groupby('Product').describe()
```
Output:

	Sales							
	count	mean	std	min	25%	50%	75%	max
Product								
Apple 2.0	232.0	152.7350 65	124.0	178.00	232.0	286.00	340.0
Dell 2.0	296.5	75.66042 6	243.0	269.75	296.5	323.25	350.0
Hp 2.0	160.0	56.56854 2	120.0	140.00	160.0	180.00	200.0

Now, this is more informative. It says a lot about the data at a glance. Individual products can also be selected: DF.GROUPBY('PRODUCT').DESCRIBE()['PRODUCT NAME E.G. 'APPLE'].

Chapter 13: Why Python for Big Data?

When it comes to the field of big data, choosing the right programming language will depend on the project. Whatever that project is, whatever the goal is, the combination of Python and Big Data is one of the most powerful.

Python is one of the most versatile programming languages in the world and also one of the easiest, allowing programmers to do far more with less code. It has plenty of scripting features and advanced libraries making it ideal for the field of data science and for big data.

5 Reasons Why Python is Best for Big Data:

Python has long been considered the best tool for big data, especially when integration between web apps and data analysis is needed And, with its library of advanced packages, it is the perfect choice for implementing many machine learning algorithms. But there are five major reasons why you should choose Python for Big Data:

1.   It's full of scientific packages

Python works for big data because of its incredibly robust library of packages, fulfilling data science and analytical needs. Some of those libraries include:

•   pandas

One of the top libraries for data analysis, pandas also gives us the data structure and operations needed for data manipulation on both numerical tables and time series.

- NumPy

NumPy is one of the fundamental Python packages that makes scientific computing possible. It has support for random number crunching, linear algebra, Fourier transforms, matrices an multi-dimensional arrays, all with help from an extensive library of mathematical functions

- SciPy

SciPy is one of the most used libraries in Big Data for technical computing and scientific computing. In it, you will find modules for:

- FFT
- Integration
- Interpolation
- Linear algebra
- ODE solvers
- Optimization
- Signal and image processing
- Special functions

And lots of other common science and engineering tasks.

- Mlpy

Mlpy is one of the machine learning libraries that works on top of SciPy and NumPy. It provides a lot of machine learning methods and helps us to find a compromise between efficiency, maintainability, usability, reproducibility, and modularity.

- Matplotlib

A popular Python library, Matplotlib helps with 2D plotting for hardcopy formats for publications. It allows us to generate error charts, histograms, bar charts, plots, scatter plots, power spectra and much more.

- Theano

Theano library is for numerical computation and helps with defining and optimizing. It also helps us with mathematical expression evaluation, potentially involving multi-dimensional arrays.

- NetworkX

The Network library is for the study of graphs, helping us in the creation, manipulation, and study of the structure, functions and dynamics of complex networks.

- SymPy

SymPy is one of the most effective libraries for symbolic computation and includes features such as:

- Basic symbolic arithmetic
- Calculus
- Algebra
- Discrete mathematics
- Quantum physics.
- Computer algebra capabilities in all different formats, such as a standalone applications, live web applications, or as a library to other applications.

- Dask

Dask is a Python big data library which helps in flexible parallel computing for analytic purpose. From the big data perspective, it works with big data collections like data frames, lists, and parallel arrays or with Python iterators for larger than the memory in a distributed environment.

- Dmelt

Otherwise known as DataMelt, this is a library or software based on Python and used in big data analysis for the statistical analysis and numeric computation of big data, not to mention its scientific visualization.

- Scikit-learn

Another popular library, scikit-learn complements SciPy and NumPy, offering features like regression, interoperability with Python libraries, and a range of clustering algorithms for gradient boosting , vector machines, DBSCAN, and random forest means.

- TensorFlow

Lastly we have TensorFlow, open source and with Python support for machine learning. The library can build and train a neural network to detect and decipher patterns, find correlations and is analogous for reasoning and learning.

2.   Compatibility with Hadoop

Because Python big data is compatible, Hadoop and big data are synonymous with one another. That means Python has compatibility with Hadoop for the purpose of working with big data. The Pydoop package in Python helps with access to the HDFI API and in writing the Hadoop MapReduce programming. Pydoop also gives the MapReduce program the ability to use the minimum amount of effort to solve some of the larger and more complex big data problems.

3.   It is Easy to Learn

Python is one of the easiest computer programming languages learn given that its features are capable of abstraction of many different things. A result of this is that programmers can get away with using fewer lines of code to achieve so much more and in a more readably way than many other languages. Aside from that, it also has scripting features. Python has plenty of user-friendly features such as simple syntax, code readability, easy implementation, and automatic data type identification and association.

4. It Has Scalability

When you are dealing with huge data scalability is incredibly important. Python is a good deal faster than other data science languages like MatLab, R, and Stata and that speed is enhance significantly with Anaconda. Because of this, Python an big data are compatible with a huge amount of flexibility and scalability.

5. Fantastic Community Support

Very often, analysis of big data will require dealing with highly complex problems and community support is invaluable in finding the solutions. As a language, Python has one of the largest and most active communities and this is great for both data scientists an programmer, offering support on all coding related issues at all levels.

Python and big data provide one of the strongest capabilities in computational terms on the platform of big data analysis. If this is your first time at data programming, Python will be a much easier language to learn than any other and is far more user-friendly.

Conclusion

Thanks for downloading this book. Let's hope it was informative and able to provide you with all of the tools you need to achieve your goals whatever they may be. Python is a powerful modern computer programming language and it is easy to learn. The syntax is simple and it allows the programmers to state their ideas in fewer lines of codes.

For you to get to this point, chances are you want to know so many things about Python, data science and so other related fields. You can be the next innovator. Building innovative technology begins with an idea, and your plan can become a reality when you make a move.

Right now, all you have to do is to imagine. Imagine how your world would be if you can take some steps to learn more about machine learning or perhaps neural networks. Imagine yourself a great data analyst who uses data science to make decisions and predictions with the use of machine learning.

Imagine having all the secrets about data science lifecycle where you can make several analyses. Imagine knowing everything about probability, statistics, fundamental, as well as data types you've read in this book. Imagine knowing all aspects of linear algebra and how you can proffer solution to many representational problems of linear algebra.

The next step is to open up your compiler and try out a few of the different things that you learned in this guidebook. The point of this guidebook is to help you learn a few more things about the Python code and to take your basic knowledge and expand it out to becoming more advanced. And the best way to do that after reading the information is to give it a try. There are a few different codes, along with various topics that we discussed in this guidebook, that you can experiment with to ensure that you are getting the most out of your coding lessons. When you are done with this guidebook, you will be better prepared to take on your own programming needs. When you are ready to take your coding to the next level, make sure to check out this guidebook to help you get started.

You have the knowledge you may need in the world of data science and Python with this book. The next step you need to take is to go out there and conquer the world.

www.ingramcontent.com/pod-product-compliance
Lightning Source LLC
Chambersburg PA
CBHW070840070326
40690CB00009B/1634